The Straight Talk
on
Parenting

St. Helena Library
1492 Library Lane
St. Helena, CA 94574
(707) 963-5244

The Straight Talk on Parenting

A No-Nonsense Approach on
How to Grow a Grown-Up

Vicki Hoefle

bibliomotion
books + media

First published by Bibliomotion, Inc.
39 Harvard Street
Brookline, MA 02445
Tel: 617-934-2427
www.bibliomotion.com

Printed in the United States of America

Library of Congress Cataloging-in-Publication Data

Hoefle, Vicki.
    The straight talk on parenting : a no-nonsense approach on how to grow a grown-up / Vicki Hoefle.
        pages cm
    Includes bibliographical references and index.
    ISBN 978-1-62956-049-6 (paperback) — ISBN 978-1-62956-050-2 (ebook) — ISBN 978-1-62956-051-9 (enhanced ebook)
    1. Parenting.   2. Child rearing.   3. Parent and child.   I. Title.
    HQ755.8.H5887 2015
    306.874—dc23
                                        2014045848

Contents

Part One
The Method

Part Two
Stories from the Heart

Foreword

When Vicki asked me to write this foreword, I was deeply honored and completely horrified. Honored because, when I met Vicki a couple of years ago, I became instantly smitten with her. Smart as hell, funny, and compassionate, Vicki immediately became someone I admired. But I was horrified because now I have to write about someone I think is great. So, I picked up a book sitting on my bedside table (a parenting book, *of course*) and started to read the foreword. It is written by the Dalai Lama. Yes, *that* Dalai Lama. I took it as a sign. Consider this foreword to be just like one the Dalai Lama would write. Me, but more like him.

In any case, I presume you have picked up this book because you want to learn more about parenting. You are in some sort of pickle with your kids and you are *tired*. Tired of the fights and the whining. Tired of the back talk and the laziness. *Tired*. When I met Vicki, I was (and still am) just like you: tired of repeating my children's names, tired of the nagging, and tired of the reminding.

I learned of *Duct Tape Parenting* from an article and thought, "This is a little nuts...I am absolutely doing this." For five days, I put a Phineas and Ferb Band-Aid over my mouth during my morning routine of getting the kids (ages two, five, and eight) up, fed, and out the door. I took pictures and wrote a blog about it, because of course it worked. Just as Vicki suggests, when we as parents take responsibility for our own behavior and, in my case, just *shut up*, we see that our children can and want to be useful, sweet, funny, caring, and *good*. And *this* is why you are going to read the second of Vicki's books, *The Straight Talk on Parenting: A No-Nonsense Approach on How to Grow a Grown-Up*.

You can read, quite literally, a million parenting books about theory and tips and tricks, etc., but this book is different because it is sustained by the belief that children are *good*, and that there are ways we can grow our families that will help us, the parents, appreciate this fact. Not only does Vicki already know this, but her book is chock-full of stories of how the model she uses looks in real families—families she has helped and who did not sugarcoat their lives for us. Because, in the end, improving our parenting is not about reading one book, but rather practicing over our lifetime. Ask Vicki about her own children and she will gleefully tell you both how they are growing *and* how she is growing as a mother. The journey isn't over! We all know this, and this book will help remind you of that fact.

So, congratulations on picking up this book. You have done yourself and your children a great service. Vicki's kindness, experience, and love for families shine through on every page; I know you will love her as much as I do.

Meghan Leahy
positivelyparenting.com/about-me/
washingtonpost.com/people/meghan-leahy

Introduction

In my first book, *Duct Tape Parenting*, I introduce parents to the concept of a less-is-more approach to raising respectful, responsible, and resilient kids. This approach ensures that parents provide opportunities for their children to participate more fully in their own lives and in the life of their family. It encourages parents to allow children to make more choices concerning daily life, so they feel a strong sense of belonging and feel valued as contributing members of their family. This less-is-more approach invites parents to show greater trust in their children and to allow them to make mistakes, take risks, and learn to navigate the real world with confidence and enthusiasm.

When I was a young mother I knew two things: first, I was not going to give my sticky-fingered toddler free rein over my home. Second, I knew that it was my responsibility to create an environment that provided plenty of practice navigating life—not just the fun stuff but the messy side as well. I knew it was my job to train my children to become resilient people who could handle whatever life threw at them.

In order to stay balanced and juggle my children's needs with my own, I created a visual to keep me focused. At first I pictured a mother standing directly in front of her children, paving the way and saving the day. I knew I did not want to be that mother. I wanted to be within reach but not in the way. So I envisioned this mother taking one step to the right and half a step back. That was the mother I wanted to be— out of direct view, but not totally out of sight. In this position, I was close enough to watch what the kids were doing without intruding. I'd be close enough to reach out and remove them from harm's way if necessary. It's from this position that I have made nearly all my parenting decisions for more than twenty years. It was a perfect balance of being involved without taking over, being active without being controlling, and demonstrating trust while including a healthy dose of caution.

When I consider our role as parents, I think about establishing an approach that supports our children as they develop healthy relationships and as they become more independent and self-reliant. This approach must also afford our kids the opportunity to practice self, social, and life skills and strengthen their ability to rebound from difficult situations with a mix of grit and resilience.

In addition to defining an approach to parenting that supports our values, preferences, and temperaments, we as parents are charged with the responsibility of sending emotionally healthy human beings into the world with a set of character traits and attributes that ensures they will become contributing members of society and thoughtful leaders, and are able to create satisfying and fulfilling lives for themselves.

In my twenty-five years working with families, I have discovered that the long-term goal of raising a healthy human being is often buried under the stress and daily grind of raising young children. Most mothers and fathers who seek out a parenting class or a parent coach to work with are looking for strategies and solutions to help them deal with an immediate challenge they are facing with one or more of their children.

In my own work with parents I can't help but encourage them to consider the bigger picture. I suggest that—although we will come up with strategies that address pesky behavior; create healthy routines for getting out of the house or to bed on time; investigate systems for organizing rooms, sports gear, and homework; develop communication styles that are respectful to everyone in the home and that maintain an attitude of cooperation and collaboration—we also need to consider the fact that we are raising future adults.

I know, as a mother and a parenting expert, that when a parent focuses on the long-term objective of raising a healthy child who will one day be an adult, many of the stressors of day-to-day life fade away. To help parents make the switch from the immediate to the long term, I ask them to participate in a simple exercise: "Let's make a list of all the character traits and attributes you hope your adult children will embody at the age of twenty-five." Parents are quick to create a long list of adjectives that include kind, responsible, respectful, hardworking, self-disciplined, happy, independent, and compassionate.

"Now, tell me the parenting strategies you are currently using to help your children develop these big, beefy, admirable qualities," I say.

There is silence, until one brave soul asks, "Does reading books to them at night or playing puzzles with them count?" I shake my head, no, and explain that those are activities that connect us to our kids, demonstrate our love for them, and help make memories, but they are not considered parenting strategies for helping our kids develop character traits.

Another parent shares, "I don't really have a strategy. What is troubling to me in this moment is that I realize I don't have any ideas for a potential strategy, and it is pretty scary to think that, as an adult and as a parent, I have no idea how to help my kids develop the very qualities that will ensure they live a happy life." This is verbatim.

It's not long before another parent in the group challenges this notion with, "Yeah, but isn't it important that we teach our kids to pick up their clothes, take their dishes to the dishwasher, clean up their rooms, take care of their gear, keep their hands to themselves, and speak to us with respect?"

And to this I answer, "Yes. It is not only important, it is imperative that we parent with both these objectives in mind. They are not in conflict with each other, and in fact there is a way to reconcile these two objectives, which can at times seem to be in a push-me, pull-you relationship with each other."

When parents finally embrace the possibility that living with a toddler and raising an adult is a reasonable proposition, there is another obstacle they must overcome: the conflict between a routine, structure, or system and the specific and unique nature of the child. This conflict is brought to light when a parent attempts to implement a strategy and experiences pushback and resistance or when a seemingly simple strategy fails to deliver any real or lasting results. It's then that I hear comments that include, "Vicki, that morning routine sounds great, but, you don't understand, it isn't going to work for my child because he is...different." Sometimes what the parents are saying is that their child is highly sensitive, easily distracted, unfocused, challenged with a learning disability, an early riser, a late sleeper, disorganized, part of a blended family, living with one parent, an only child, a child diagnosed with a hyperactivity disorder, and so on. And sometimes it's just a sense that their child is not going to respond well to the strategy being presented. This is the intuitive nature of parenting, and it is the reason that all parents must consider their child's unique personality when designing any routine or structure or implementing boundaries and limits.

From here, I help parents integrate these two seemingly opposing ideas by showing them how to adapt any routine, structure, boundary, or limit so that it supports the intuitive knowledge they have about their child. It goes without saying that I acknowledge that every child is different, and in fact every family member is different; however, the method I have been using, and the one I am sharing with you in this book, works for exactly this reason. It takes into account the unique nature of the child in the creation and integration of any routine. I acknowledge that parenting is not a cookie-cutter proposition, and that by exercising a little creativity and experimentation it is possible to modify and design a system that will support the unique child you are raising.

At first it may seem like a big task—to overhaul the thinking behind our parenting decisions and commit to a new method for raising kids—but you'll find that once you open up to the possibilities (and combine it with the foundation from *Duct Tape Parenting*), it is possible and yes, enjoyable. In fact, there is new energy, hope, motivation, and excitement that come when you learn to parent a child while raising a future adult. You learn the art of balancing routines, systems, and structures that will support a busy family life, obligations, and the uniqueness and spirit of your child.

I followed my intuition most of the time. You have this inside you as well. Listen to that internal voice that says, *there has to be a better way than being here, down the rabbit hole, over and over again.* There is. Listen to that voice even as you are learning and following the method I lay out for you, and you will soon find that you have an approach to parenting that supports your family through all of the growing pains, developmental phases, life changes, and surprise events that greet anyone raising children in the twenty-first century.

It is my hope that this book reflects the ease and value of parenting with the future in mind. It is also my goal to encourage you, the parent, to have confidence in your intuition—that gut feeling—that your child may or may not need certain structures and boundaries, routines, and so forth. When you stay focused on the child and your family's values, the path becomes much clearer. You stop listening to all the parenting tips and tricks and ideas and trends, and you stay steady toward your goal: raising a child who will be skilled, both socially and emotionally, as an adult. Once you recognize the method in the madness, everything becomes systematic and smooth.

I encourage you to stick with this. Take it slow. Listen to your internal voice. I hope that after reading just a few stories from other parents who traded "wing it" parenting for methodical, intentional parenting, you will find yourself inspired to join us. Within each chapter, you'll read stories from parents who have been successful at balancing long-term with short-term objectives and using their intuition in collaboration with traditional systems, strategies, and routines for raising children. Use this book as a reference and come back to it as you, your children, and your family grow and change. It can remind you where you have been and how much progress you have made, and will inspire you to keep going.

PART ONE

The Method

It is not unusual for parents to describe my knack for getting to the heart of a family problem as a "gift" or a mysterious talent. Whether the difficulty is sleeping issues, nonstop sibling battles, or power struggles that escalate into tantrums, I offer a course of action that is simple, manageable, and relevant to the family I am working with. Parents are shocked when they realize that the immediate relief they feel also produces a long-term positive change in the overall family dynamic. The truth is, it's not a gift, it's a cultivated talent, an intentional training, and a method I have been using for more than twenty years. It's a plan any parent can follow (including you!).

Parents find it hard to believe that as a "parent educator" I could find myself distracted or depleted, stressed out, tapped out, spent, confused, perplexed, or bewildered in my own parenting journey, but I did and I still do from time to time. I am no different from any other parent. The difference is, however, that I had a long-term plan, a strategy to follow that kept me from steering too far off my intended track.

The method I have been using with my own children and in my work with families for the past twenty-five years can be taught and mastered by parents who are looking to create a more peaceful, enjoyable, stable, and sustainable home life for themselves and their kids. All you need are the basic elements of the method, time to practice, a commitment to the process, and a willingness to go through the trial-and-error phase and make small adjustments so that the method feels authentic and natural to you and your family.

As each season ushers in a new lineup of classes and workshops, more moms and dads are filling the rooms or working with me privately. Why, with so many parenting books on the shelves and so many online resources offering child-rearing advice, are more parents making the time to work with a parenting expert? When I ask them, they tell me that they want more confidence and clarity when it comes to making their parenting decisions. They are tired of flip-flopping through strategies that don't deliver on the promise of bringing more peace and happiness into their lives with kids. And many parents are now talking to friends who have older children and are reporting that they would have done things very differently if they'd realized early on that the goal was not to produce a polite seven-year-old but to raise a high-functioning, emotionally healthy adult. Parents work with me because they are frustrated by not having a plan for dealing with the daily challenges that arise when raising kids in a fast-paced, ever-changing, pressure-cooker culture and because they are afraid that their adult children won't make it on their own.

That's why I needed a simple method that both addressed the daily challenges of living with children and ensured I would raise healthy adults. Having such a plan brought a sense of calm, confident resolve into my life as a parent. And it can do the same for you.

Fundamentals

It would be impossible for me to talk about the method I use to identify family challenges and possible solutions without first taking a moment to talk about the fundamental themes that run through all of my work.

I truly believe that almost every challenge we face with a child can be traced back to:

- A fracture in the relationship we have with our child, which manifests itself in the form of increased power struggles, a sense of disconnection between parents and their children, and an overall atmosphere of frustration and stress in our day-to-day lives

- A child whose efforts to become independent have been thwarted, and thus she is too dependent on a parent and is improperly trained to take on the tasks of life
- Or both

These central themes influence every decision I make when I am in the presence of children, whether they are my own or someone else's. The question I ask myself every time I am interacting with a child is this: "Is what I am about to do going to enhance a healthy relationship with this child and boost his ability to become independent and self-reliant?" Only when I can answer yes to this question, am I willing to speak or act. Those who practice the concepts that make up my work will testify that these are hallmarks of my philosophy.

In this book, I dive deeper into the importance of relationships and offer parents a chance to help their children develop a relationship blueprint that will guide them toward healthy relationships and away from unhealthy ones. Along with the relationship blueprint, I include a number of strategies parents can utilize to foster independence in their children no matter what their age. Beyond that, I use the method to:

- Identify the challenge quickly so parents can put their energy into finding solutions instead of getting weighed down by details of the drama
- Identify strategies to get through a "red zone" moment that will move the action forward without making things worse
- Identify adult character traits that will help ensure that parents raise children who are ready to take on the challenges and wonders of adult life
- Design routines, structures, boundaries, and limits in combination with a child's unique nature to achieve the perfect blend of freedom and order

Once parents understand the method and are given a chance to practice it, they are able to enjoy a more relaxed and confident attitude about their parenting and focus their efforts on the journey as well as the destination.

The Elements

There are four elements that make up the method I use to identify family challenges and brainstorm solutions to bring about long-term, sustainable change. Each of the four elements can be used separately, but when they are used in combination with each other, families transform in remarkable ways.

Relationship blueprint: In *Duct Tape Parenting*, I shared with readers the two decisions that I made as a young mother. First, that I was not willing to fight with my kids for eighteen years; this meant that, second, I would have to spend time cultivating a respectful, honest, and loving relationship with them in order to minimize potential power struggles and a long-term fracture in our relationship. As the result of those two decisions, I developed an entire parenting approach that focused more on maintaining, growing, and cultivating healthy relationships than on having kids who were neat, tidy, polite, and compliant. It made life with my own five kids fun, satisfying, and, believe it or not, mostly peaceful and harmonious.

I knew firsthand that investing in the relationship with my kids would significantly decrease the power struggles, help us all get out of the house on time (after all it takes real cooperation to move a family of seven out the door each morning without tears or tantrums), and reduce the daily stress of living in a fast-paced world. Beyond that I began to understand that everything my children learned about relationships would come from the one they were establishing with me, their mother. With that realization came a commitment to helping my kids design a relationship blueprint that would ensure they knew the difference between a healthy and an unhealthy relationship and would be drawn to individuals who modeled healthy relationship qualities.

I accepted that my job was to model for my kids what a healthy relationship looked like, sounded like, and felt like, as a way to ensure that they had a better chance of entering into a healthy relationship with someone outside of their family. This is why the first element of my method focuses first on the relationship we have with our children—because whether we want to accept it or not, in every moment we are either interfering with or enhancing the relationship we have with our kids. This is a theme in parenting that cannot go overlooked. A healthy relationship with our kids increases our chances that those other problem areas either aren't problems or they are so small that we can deal with them easily, swiftly, and effectively.

Fostering independence: The second element is the idea that we are responsible for helping our kids develop the independence and self-reliance they need to manage life on their own. It's part of our job to help them feel confident in their ability to handle anything life throws their way. On a small scale, this means allowing our children to master self, home, social, and life skills.

Beyond that, fostering our children's independence makes it more likely that they will have the skills necessary to navigate a world that is overly connected in some ways and disconnected in others. As children's exposure to a larger world beyond their neighborhoods and communities expands and their access to technology increases, parents' concern about their children's safety rises. The natural tendency is to overprotect, and that leads to an attitude of "keeping the kids young and innocent for as long as possible." Unfortunately, this puts our children at greater risk. The more empowered our children feel, the more capable they believe they are; the more experience they have in making inconsequential choices when they are young, the more confident we will be in their ability to make thoughtful, wise, and safe choices when they are exposed to the larger and sometimes more dangerous world.

Living with a toddler, raising an adult: The third element is reconciling the idea that we can implement a strategy to deal with a frustrated three-year-old and at the same moment foster character traits that will assist our twenty-three-year old in his life as an adult. Although these two ideas, living with a toddler and raising an adult, seem to be at odds with each other, the truth is, they can live together harmoniously. With a bit of practice and commitment you will experience the same awe-inspiring results that I, as a mother raising five children, and the tens of thousands of parents I've worked with have experienced.

When you spend as much time helping your kids develop character traits as you do learning a technique to deal with bedtimes, back talk, and fighting, the daily challenges of life start to, dare I say it, disappear. When a child begins to develop self-control, a trait we want our adult children to embody, he can manage his impulse to pummel his younger brother for knocking down his blocks. You no longer need a strategy for the moment because the strategy is his newfound self-control. I, for one, found great satisfaction in knowing that fostering a character trait in my child would make a discipline strategy unnecessary.

Intention meets intuition: And finally, the fourth element combines following your gut feeling, or even the patterns you recognize in your kids, with incorporating routines, structures, boundaries, and limits that ensure the entire family can function in a fast-paced world. It's a balancing act, to be sure, but when intuition and structure are integrated successfully, you suddenly have a morning routine that has everyone up, dressed, fed, and smiling as you start your day. And, this isn't just momentary magic. This is the magic that comes from designing an intentional plan with the unique nature of your kids in mind.

Often, when I am teaching a class and introducing the idea of routines, parents find it difficult to accept because they assume I mean a generic, one-size-fits-all option. Before they even process the idea that each system is tailored to each family or family member, they say, "It won't work." I encourage you to keep an open mind, and if I use an example that won't work for your family, consider reworking the routine into something that looks appropriate for you and your kids. Your values drive everything you do. My values are different. That's why I've included so many stories from real families. The trick is to take the nugget of structure or stability and tweak it into a solution for your child.

This is where the magic (and fun!) is. You start to recognize ways to create the perfect blend of structure and personal preference. Take some time to consider the benefits and then give it a try. Use this rock-solid, time-tested method, and make it work for your family. When you do this, you've found your true north. As a result, you will feel that confidence and clarity you are looking for to guide your family today and into the future.

CHAPTER ONE

From Footprints to Blueprints

A child is an active and dynamic entity.... Children develop their relationships to others through the use of their own creative powers and their ingenuity in trying to find their place. A child will try something: if it works and if it fits in with his goal, he retains it as a method of finding his personal identity. Sometimes the child may discover that the same technique fails to work with all people. Now he has two courses open to him. He can either retreat or refuse to cooperate with such a person, or he can use a new technique and develop an entirely different relationship.
—Rudolf Dreikurs, *Children: The Challenge*

Have you ever considered that the relationship you establish with your child, which begins at birth, becomes the blueprint for every other relationship she enters into during the course of her life?

If you are like many of the parents I have worked with over the past twenty-five years, you haven't. It's more likely that you thought about what kind of mother or father you would be and the responsibilities that go along with raising a child from infancy to adulthood. You might have imagined the relationship you would have with your child and vowed that for you there would be no yelling in the market, plenty of patience with him as he struggled to tie his shoes, and calm and respectful talk about homework and teachers. You might have recalled your own childhood with fond memories and wanted to base your parenting on the way you were raised. On the other hand, you might have found your own childhood somewhat distasteful and made the decision to do things very differently when you got to be a parent. In either case, it's rare to find parents who truly understand the correlation between the relationship they establish with their very young child and the impact this relationship has on all of their child's future relationships with family members and others.

Our children are part of a social world that is built around and depends upon relationships. In an attempt to find their place in their first and primary social structure, they watch, assess, learn, and then experiment with different ways of interacting and engaging with their caregivers. Now consider that young children cannot differentiate between healthy or unhealthy relationships. If they aren't taught how to distinguish between the two and what qualities are present in healthy relationships, it's reasonable to think they might very well find themselves in dysfunctional ones through no fault of their own. Although children may not understand the meaning of the word *relationship*, they are still experiencing, discovering, testing, and learning, and it isn't long before they begin to mimic their parents' language, tones, attitudes, and behaviors, giving us a first glimpse into how our children anchor their experiences and apply them in developing their very own personal relationship blueprint.

Once created, a child's relationship blueprint is used to help navigate most, if not all, future relationships, including those with grandparents, aunts and uncles, cousins, and family friends. She will look to her relationship blueprint as she learns to navigate her first playgroup or day care, or her preschool or kindergarten classroom, and it will become even more important as your child's world expands and she is required to navigate relationships with her classmates, teachers, and coaches through elementary, middle, and high school, and beyond.

What Is a Blueprint?

Imagine the blueprints to a house. What does an ideal home look like to you? Imagine the sketches on paper. This blueprint of your home contains the structure for your vision, along with all the specific design elements that reflect your style, taste, and preferences. The blueprint acts as an anchor and allows you to build the house of your dreams. It has been carefully mapped and measured. Are we going to use birch or maple, granite or stone? Deviations can mean unexpected costs, delayed timelines, or safety issues, so it's crucial to follow the blueprint or you'll end up with something other than what you envisioned. Shortcuts and on-the-spot upgrades can be tempting when you're in the middle of a build, but knowing that the final outcome may be affected makes sticking to the plan worthwhile.

Now consider a relationship blueprint. What does an ideal relationship look like to you, and what goes into the relationship of your dreams? Like a structural blueprint, a relationship blueprint serves as a map to the end goal: a solid, sound relationship. Am I going to use encouraging words or criticism? Indulge in my tendency to yell or use a respectful speaking voice? Will I pull out the sarcasm or remain sincere in my attitude? When we interact with our kids, we are either following the plans to ensure we reach our goal or we are making on-the-spot changes because it's faster, we're tired, and we're wondering, "What difference will it make if I cut a few corners?"

Here's the kicker: the interactions—each and every one of them—between parent and child are the basis for the child's relationship blueprint, which she will use to evaluate all future relationships. What we choose to put on that "map" affects how our children move on and interact with others. I believe that if more parents understood this, they would take the time to make complete and intentional blueprints; often they don't, simply because life gets in the way and they build as they go. In the world of construction, this is a recipe for disaster. The same goes for parenting.

Reflecting on Your Relationship Blueprint

Think back to your own childhood. You likely have strong memories of your parents and the way they spoke to you and to each other, how they made you feel in their company, how they handled your mischievous behavior, and how they supported your interests. You may recall specific facial expressions they used to communicate their disappointment or approval, a certain tone of voice they used to get your attention, a particular mood they displayed when they were tired or stressed, or the way they used their sense of humor to cut through tension.

Likewise, their parenting style—which might have included hovering or trusting, criticizing or encouraging, and physical gestures of affection or aggression as well as expressions of friendliness or frustration—influenced your ideas about relationships and perhaps, without knowing it, swayed your decision to enter into a deeper relationship with your parents or distance yourself from them when possible.

When you got older, you widened your observations to relatives and eventually to friends and lovers, and you took note of how these people interacted with you and with others. Perhaps they included you or ignored you, spoke down to you or asked curious questions about your life, displayed a good disposition or appeared distant, aloof, and uninterested. All of these experiences influenced your relationship blueprint. Whatever your reaction was—trust, resilience, resentment, or retreat, or any other—you internalized it and made your own map accordingly. Along the way, you undoubtedly encountered people who were accepting or critical, flexible or rigid, demanding or cooperative, honest or deceitful. All of these further influenced your ideas about relationships and cemented the kinds of people you wanted to surround yourself with and those you wanted to steer clear of.

Our children will be building relationships for the rest of their lives, and so it seems reasonable that we'd take the time to design a solid relationship for them to learn from. This means that, instead of spending our time investing in superficial and temporary parenting decisions (like nursery colors, the perfect preschool, or the outfits our kids wear), we can best spend our time building a solid blueprint for all future relationships. This means paying attention to our word choices, discipline decisions, tone of voice, comments and criticisms, and so on. It means that we take the time to be intentional, aware, and respectful in a way that stays true to a plan and its solid outcomes.

Recognizing Healthy Relationships

Think of all the positive relationships you've had or witnessed in your lifetime. Consider the trust, love, empathy, cooperation, respect, and honest communication present in those relationships. Imagine the relationship you would like to have with your child. In a perfect world, what would this ideal relationship look like? How would you treat each other?

Select words that fit your concept of an ideal relationship from the list below and write them down in your notes. Add other words that you associate with a loving, engaging, satisfying relationship. Refer to your unique list to keep you on track in your relationship with your children.

Mutual respect	Support	Compassion
Trust	Kindness	Consistency
Flexibility	Boundaries	Integrity
Loyalty	Listening	Radical faith
Appreciation	Empathy	Cooperation
Acceptance	Love	Honesty
Understanding	Affection	

Recognizing Unhealthy Relationships

Now, do the same exercise for unhealthy relationships that you did for healthy ones: think of the worst relationships you've experienced or witnessed. Envision the cycles of hurt and betrayal, anger and disrespect, manipulation and judgment, and the unhealthy communication usually present in these relationships. Then, in a worst-case scenario, think about what a fractured relationship with your would child entail. Circle the biggies below and add more words to this list. Get every negative relationship indicator down on paper. Then you'll know where to steer clear as you work on building a healthy relationship with your child.

Authoritarian behavior	Belittling	Dishonesty
Nagging	Shaming/ humiliation	Grudge holding
Disappointment	Taking advantage	Worthlessness
Judgment	Trust breaking	Inconvenience
Passive-aggressiveness	Unethical actions	Insignificance
Guilt tripping	Rigid standards	Arrogance
	Double standards	Control

Whether we are modeling healthy relationship attributes or unhealthy ones, our kids are watching and learning. In all likelihood they will seek out partners who make them feel like we do, so it's in our children's best interest for us to give serious consideration to our daily interactions with them.

Healthy from the Inside Out

As a start, it's helpful to recognize that the activities we do and the time we spend with our children don't equate to a child's ability to create a healthy relationship blueprint. Loving our children, reading to them, spending time with them, or bonding with them over a movie or special vacation is not the same as building a healthy relationship with them. In fact, it could be argued that it is during the times of stress, unrest, disagreements, and power struggles that children are truly learning what constitutes a healthy or unhealthy relationship. Building a good relationship blueprint is not about having a happy, positive experience all the time. Testing the relationship and working through the tough stuff is what teaches a child how to handle the ups and downs that life will surely send her way! In these very real moments, children begin fitting together the pieces that will ultimately make up their personal blueprint for most if not all of their future relationships.

No parent I know wants to end his day with a feeling of regret, remorse, or resentment, but unfortunately many parents do. They question their parenting decisions, question their children's behavior, and question whether life with kids will be the satisfying experience they dreamed it would be before their children arrived. Taking the time to understand the power of the relationship blueprint will help bring a sense of confidence, courage, and, ultimately, calm as you make the changes necessary to positively influence your child's ability to enter healthy relationships later in life.

Three Mistaken Messages

Even if you are a parent who can articulate the idea of a relationship blueprint, it's still a challenge to identify all the ways in which we unintentionally and inadvertently muck things up. Over the past twenty-five years, I have identified three specific ways that well-intentioned parents accidentally influence the relationship blueprint design in less than positive ways:

1. Labels that belittle: Labeling our kids with negative attributes, which influences their self-image
2. If you loved me, you would change for me: Using parenting strategies to "get" children to behave teaches children that it is acceptable to use whatever means are necessary to get people to change for them
3. Words that wound: Proclaiming specific values as important to us and then demonstrating them in ways that do not align with the true definition of the word

Message One – Labels That Belittle

What is the impact on our children when they are bombarded with comments like, "You noodle," "You are disorganized," "You never follow through," "You have to be more responsible," "You should be more respectful," "You are so impatient," and "Will you always need me to help you?" These words, these attitudes, and our propensity to constantly "work" on our kids as if they are projects that need improvement guarantees that the image they first construct of themselves will be based on the words, attitudes, and areas of correction we bombard them with on any given day.

The following stories illustrate how "feeding the weed" (focusing on pesky behavior) and labeling our children with negative character traits interferes with their ability to enter into and maintain a healthy relationship with anyone outside their family. Although these may seem like extreme examples, they are typical of the many parents I work with who are struggling to break old patterns in their behavior.

Overwhelmed and Sensitive – Judy H.

I was the kid who was easily overwhelmed. My parents referred to me as being overly sensitive, and they made sure that they paved the way for me by removing obstacles so that I wouldn't get overwhelmed. Now, as an adult, I still experience myself as easily overwhelmed, and if I am not careful, I expect the people closest to me to make my life as easy as they can. Truthfully, if I feel like I am not going to handle a situation well, I will use my "label" to manipulate people into letting me off the hook or making excuses for me. If that doesn't work I will avoid difficult situations and people altogether. Eventually, people tire of my neediness and inability to deal with the challenges of life. Quite often I am initially attracted to people who will make my life easier, but I soon tire of being treated like a child and break off the relationship. Either way, the relationship ends.

You Can't Make Me – Jarrod L.

I was the kid who refused to take orders from anyone. Any direct command from my parents was met with defiance and the guarantee that I would do the opposite. Because they didn't know what to do with me, they gave in, and to this day I still refuse to "do what I am told." In school I earned the title of "chronically disruptive student" in the classroom and bully on the playground. As you can imagine, this idea I have of myself is a real challenge in both my professional and personal life. My unwillingness to cooperate with people has resulted in numerous failed personal relationships and jobs where I am repeatedly passed over when it's time for promotions. At twenty-six I am finally learning how to cooperate, but it is slow going.

Criticism and Blame –Tyrus A.

I was the kid who always seemed to disappoint his parents. They were never satisfied with anything I did. They thought that criticizing me would help me do better, but it did the opposite. Now, as a grown man, I don't do things that I think leave me open to criticism or will let people down. I apologize for things that are not my responsibility, blame myself when things don't go well, and am hesitant to try new things. Relationships? I am a disaster at relationships. I wait for criticism and when I meet someone who notices the best in me, I don't believe them. It's not long before the game of "lift Gabe up" loses its appeal and the person moves on. I have been called "Eeyore" more times than I care to admit.

As I said, these may sound like extreme examples, but more and more adults are beginning to trace the challenges they face in their adult relationships back to their early childhood experiences, and more specifically to the relationship blueprint they created as kids.

By shifting our focus and recognizing that our kids are in the process of developing the kinds of behaviors, values, and character traits that will assist them during every phase of life, we can more thoughtfully and intentionally help them develop the kind of self-image that will make it possible for them to become people who respect themselves in the deepest and most honest way. I'll tell you how to turn this around later in the chapter.

Message Two – If You Loved Me, You'd Change

The second message that contributes to the development of our child's relationship blueprint is based on in-the-moment, not-sure-what-else-to-do strategies, which include the nagging, reminding, lecturing, saving, bribing, coaxing, controlling, punishing, and shaming many parents use to try to manipulate their children into behaving.

As parents, when we focus on fixing or changing our children's pesky behaviors, we teach them that this is an acceptable relationship model. Our children interact with others thinking, "I don't like some of your behaviors, so I am going to try to change you to suit my liking." Our children grow up to believe that if the people they are in relationship with really cared about them, they would indeed be willing to change for them. Now, that is not to say that we don't want to assist our children in developing behaviors that will support them as individuals and in their relationships with others, but how we go about doing that either contributes to an unhealthy view of relationships or a healthy one.

Criticize and Demand – Tina H.

My relatives told me that I was a very precocious and confident young child who gave my parents a run for their money. My parents had very strong views on the way children should behave, how they should do in school, and how a house should run. They used constant criticism and comparisons to get me to toe the line. I think I made the decision when I was still very young that when I was an adult, if people didn't do what I wanted, I would do the same thing to them that my parents were doing to me. I would criticize them until they gave in to my demands.

One of my first adult experiences was renting an old house with several girls from school. After a few months, one of my new roommates started to get on my nerves because I didn't like the way she cleaned the kitchen. After all, there is really only one way to clean a kitchen. Instead of talking to her about it and working out a system that would support both our personalities and habits, I started to criticize the way she loaded the dishwasher and took jabs at her for leaving the pots and pans out to "air dry." When none of that worked to get her to clean the kitchen the way I wanted her to, I extended the criticism to other areas of her life and I started to compare her to our other roommates. Two months later she told me she was moving out. This is a pattern in my life. I am doing to other people what my parents did to me. I know how irritating it is, because I experienced it firsthand, but that doesn't change the fact that I don't have skills or the experience to communicate honestly with people who have a different style than I do.

Nag, Nag, Nag – Linda R.

My parents weren't all that heavy-handed, but they nagged and reminded and directed us until we got old enough to get in the car and drive away. I didn't realize I had adopted those same tactics until a friend pointed out how I spoke to my girl-friend. She said I sounded like her mother, not her girlfriend. Although I was mortified, I also knew she was bang on. The problem was, I had no idea how to change my behavior because my role models were my parents. I was doing what they did. Vicki has a saying, "Children don't grow out of, they grow into whatever it is they are doing at the moment or what they are most often exposed to," and in this case she hit the bull's-eye.

These stories illustrate how children conclude that, when they are in a relationship with someone who behaves in a way they deem unaccept-able, they have every right to nag, remind, threaten, exclude, ignore, hurt, or punish the person in order to get him to change. These are the skills the child has witnessed, experienced, and practiced during his young life. The children are doing what they know. Yes, it is that cut-and-dry. Just watch a group of five-year-olds playing and you will hear quite clearly the words they have been hearing at home and how they have interpreted them and applied them in designing their relationship blueprint.

- "That's not how you are supposed to build a sand castle. You do it like this."
- "If you want to play with us you will have to ask us nicely or we won't play with you."
- "Are you going to use red to color your flower? I think it would look better in yellow.
- Are you sure you want to put the house there? Wouldn't it look better over there? I've never seen a window like that. They usually look like this."
- "Stop acting like a baby. It didn't hurt that much."
- "Ya know, people aren't going to be friends with you if you don't..."

Message Three – Words That Wound

Just using words to define a healthy relationship isn't enough to ensure that our kids actually understand the true definition of the words we are using. As parents, it is our responsibility to model and live in harmony with our values, so our kids can experience firsthand what those values look and feel like in relationship with other people.

Most adults will admit that how and what we communicate, whether verbal or nonverbal, is the foundation for all our relationships, healthy or unhealthy. Communication begins with the words we use, words like respect, cooperation, responsibility, compassion, love, acceptance, and integrity. These words are the foundation for all communication, but as I said earlier, the words alone have no meaning for our children. The words take on meaning through action. When a parent uses the word "respect" at the same time she is yelling at a child, has her hands on her hips, or is shooting nasty looks across the room, the child mistakenly interprets the word respect based on those actions.

If parents are not careful to consistently demonstrate the true meaning behind their words, it's unlikely our kids will have much luck in accurately ascribing meaning to those words.

Respect: Maybe you recognize yourself in some of these all too common phrases:

- "You aren't really going to wear that to school are you?
- "Why do you put so much butter on your toast?"
- "Go tell your brother you are sorry and wipe that look off of your face!"
- "No, I am not giving you a choice, just go get in the car, now!"
- "Who do you think you are talking to, young man?"
- "I know I said you could have James over to play, but I changed my mind and that's that."
- "I wouldn't be yelling at you if you hadn't been so clumsy and dropped the eggs all over the floor."
- "No, you can't help me in the shop. I don't have time to watch you every minute and you are likely to hurt yourself if I don't."
- "Can't you just go find something to do for five minutes without badgering me for something?"
- "I would never have spoken to my mother in that tone of voice. If I had, I would have been on restriction for two weeks."

Message: Respect is a one-way street (my street).

If you are thinking that these comments sound harsh, you are right. And yet this is just a sampling of the ways in which we communicate with our children that in no way reflects a respectful attitude or communication style. Take some time to listen to the way you speak to your children and ask yourself if you would pass the "true meaning of the word respect" test.

Cooperation: Do the following statements sound like people cooperating with each other?

- "Put your coat on, keep your hands to yourself, and don't ask me for anything when we get to the checkout counter."
- "Just sit still so I can get these boots on you."
- "I know you wanted the other backpack, but it was cheap. This one will last all year."
- "Why don't you sit there and sing me a song while I bake the cake? Then there won't be a big mess to clean up.

- "It's faster if I do this myself."
- "No, you may not, and there is nothing to discuss."

Message: Cooperation means do what I say, when I say it.

Responsibility: Maybe you have never made these statements to your children, but you've probably heard another parent on the playground speak to his child this way:

- "It's your responsibility to remember your homework, so this is the last time I am going to bring it to you."
- "I just don't understand you. I will carry your backpack from the car, but you are old enough to be responsible for your things."
- "I put your mittens in your backpack, how can you keep losing track of them?"
- "I'm going to call the coach and ask him why he is being so hard on you at practice."
- "I think the teacher should understand what a tough time you are having right now and excuse some of your late assignments."
- "You shouldn't be expected to remember all of your belongings with your busy schedule."

Message: You are not capable of being responsible for your things or yourself.

Three Intentional Messages

If we know what *not* to do, then it's time to find out what we *can* do to ensure that our children have the best chance at creating a healthy relationship blueprint. If it's true that the labels we use to describe our child's less-than-exemplary behavior (noodling, whining, defiance, laziness, moodiness) and the techniques we use to try to change their behavior (threatening, nagging, punishing, doing for, saving, excusing) influence their relationship blueprint in unhealthy ways, then the solution is to shift our focus, model healthy relationship dynamics, and watch healthy relationship attributes take shape. Likewise, the way we demonstrate the words we use to describe a healthy relationship influences our children's relationship blueprint in significant ways, so it's imperative that we pay close attention to our responses and reactions and challenge ourselves to stay true to the real definition of the words we use with our kids.

If our goal is to ensure that our children have the best chance at designing a healthy relationship blueprint, it's as simple as this:

1. Labels That Lift: Drop the negative labels and focus on strengths. It's just as easy to say, "You are tenacious" as it is to say, "You are stubborn"; or to say, "You have leadership skills" rather than "You are bossy," or, "You are thoughtful about your morning routine" rather than "You are such a dawdler." Highlighting and spotlighting strengths in our kids helps them develop a strong and healthy self-ideal, and this will influence every aspect of their relationship blueprint.

2. Tools of the Trade: Send the message that you love your children as they are and you will not use shady tactics (clandestine parenting strategies) to manipulate them into changing. Instead, you will model ways in which two very different people can be who they are and accept others for who they are. It is our responsibility to communicate to our children that change is initiated from inside, from a desire to change for yourself and not for someone else, and that requiring someone to change as a way of demonstrating love for you qualifies as manipulative and abusive behavior.

3. The Truth in Our Words: If you want your children to show respect, they must understand the true meaning of the word and they learn this by watching you. We are charged with adequately representing the true meaning of the words we use with our kids in order to ensure that our children can live them honestly and recognize them in relationship with others.

Message One – Labels That Lift

Let's dive deeper into the idea of labels and how our children build their self-ideal around the words their parents use to describe them. In the following stories, adults share their memories of childhood and how their parents supported their growth and influenced their relationship blueprint.

Tenacity and Grit – Amy J.

I am one of three girls. My sisters and I know that our parents made a concerted effort to raise strong women. They repeatedly used words like tenacious, gracious, and levelheaded. When you are a kid, you don't necessarily pay attention to the words themselves, as much as you start to notice what behavior your parents ascribe to the word. It shaped the way we saw ourselves and influenced the kinds of people we were drawn toward. I don't remember my parents dwelling on our less-than-desirable behavior, and as a result I don't tend to dwell on personality traits I don't necessarily admire in others. My parents accepted us for who we were and we girls try to do the same. We all have a tenacious spirit, although our levels of tenacity vary. We can stick with things, even when it's hard, and that applies to academics, sports, or any other area of life. In our relationships, that means that we are willing to work through the rough areas. I think graciousness was the counterbalance to our tenacity. My mom was an approachable and inviting person, and I think a gracious person embodies those qualities. It's important to all of us that people are comfortable in our presence. My parents were great role models for levelheaded behavior and they acknowledged when the three of us were drawing on that strength in situations that might warrant a more dramatic response, like an unexpected pimple right before prom.

Growing into Respect – Paul K.

I don't remember my parents ever asking for or demanding that I show them respect. What I do recall is that they made it a point to acknowledge when I was being respectful. I heard things like "Thanks for respecting the fact that I like the pantry organized a certain way" and "It takes a lot of self-respect to ..." and "It's easy to say yes to your request to use my tools, because you are so respectful with them." Now, I am going to guess that I probably wasn't as respectful as they led me to believe, but because they pointed out all the times that I was showing even a modicum of respect, I grew into an adult who values respect. More importantly, they modeled respect for themselves by creating clear boundaries about what they would and would not do in terms of their parenting and modeled respect toward me by being consistent and including me in family decision making. As an adult, I can tell by the end of an evening who I will choose to spend more time with based almost solely on their level of respect for self and others.

Square Peg in a Square Hole – Caroline C.

I was born into a very gregarious and athletic family. Unfortunately, I am cautious by nature, and saying I am a bookworm is an understatement. Instead of my parents pushing me to conform or comparing me to my siblings or making me feel guilty because I didn't value the same "seize the day" attitude they embodied, they encouraged and supported who I was innately. They identified traits in me that could easily have been overlooked or undervalued. Words like "thoughtful" and "calm" replaced words like "introverted" and "scared," which carried negative connotations in our clan. I had a wicked sense of humor, even as a young kid, and a huge vocabulary, and they pointed out how these traits added value to our lives as a family. I never felt that they were putting me down; instead, they showed me how important these traits are in a well-rounded relationship. As an adult,

I am much more adventurous as a result of not being pushed by my parents and I have a keen sense of who I am, and I am a bulldog about staying true to my natural rhythms and preferences. I have been known to end a first date well before dessert if I get the sense that the other person doesn't accept me for who I am.

Straight Talk

This is what it sounds like when a parent focuses on strengths and spotlights healthy relationship qualities:

- "You showed a lot of **patience** with your brother tonight. I know you wanted to work on the Legos alone, but you were **kind** enough to let him join you."
- "I know how much **courage** it took to tell Nancy you didn't want to go out with her anymore. You showed her a lot of **respect** by talking to her in person and not calling her on the phone, which would have been easier."
- "Sometimes it's hard to **forgive** people when they break your trust, but it's clear this **friendship** is important to you and you were willing to stick with it and work things out.
- "Your **tenacity** paid off on the field today. All those extra hours of practice made the difference in the final score."
- "You are really **determined** to pour just the right amount of milk on that cereal."
- "You **rebound** so quickly when things don't go your way."

When you speak this way, it is reasonable to think that you will raise a child who feels adequate and sees the best not only in himself but also in others.

Message: You are valuable (even though we do things differently).

Message Two – Tools of the Trade

Beyond the labels we use with our children are the strategies we use to communicate the "how" of relationships. A healthy set of tools, demonstrated by thoughtful parents, will be the difference between children who believe they have a right to ask others to change for them and children who look for ways to work cooperatively with others.

Trained in Collaboration – Julia P.

My parents were both mediators, and, as a result, they brought their skills in collaboration to our lives. When I was just a toddler, my parents spent time talking with me about where I wanted to keep my clothes and where to put the bed and whether I wanted a light on when I went to sleep. It wasn't that I could even answer any of their questions or participate in these discussions, but I felt included and I felt valued from the time I was very small. Over time, I learned how to hold my own and fight for what I wanted, and I learned to hear my parents out and at times accept their wisdom. When I got older I was invited and encouraged to help create family policies and explore the ramifications of those policies. I learned how to argue respectfully, listen attentively, and consider different points of view. Now, it has been said that as an adult I can be too subdued and matter-of-fact in my daily interactions, but I assure you that my passion is there. The difference is, it is focused on things that matter to me. I do not look to overpower people or to manipulate them into doing what I want.

Think Before You Speak – Max D.

As an adult, I get along really well with people. I am not interested in trying to get people to change for me and I am not easily manipulated into changing for others, and there is no mystery as to why. My mom and dad parented with a simple motto: "Say what you mean, mean what you say, and then do it."

- **Say what you mean:** This meant they had to think before they spoke. They couldn't just throw out random consequences or answer our questions without first thinking about them. I am clear with people about what I want and what I don't want, what I will and will not do, what bothers me and what delights me. I take responsibility for being clear with others so there are very few misunderstandings in my relationships.
- **Mean what you say:** This meant that you should be ready to fight for what you believe. They told us that this demonstrated to their kids that not only was there thought behind what they said, but that they were willing to fight for their position, so if we wanted to challenge it, we better bring our A game. I stand behind what I say and if I make a mistake I am the first to admit it and to make amends. I don't threaten people or use tears to get what I want. This keeps the drama out of my relationships and I tend to attract people who are very emotionally healthy.
- **Do it:** This is all about follow-through. And I have the courage and the confidence to follow through with what I say. It can be tough, but in the long run, it's worth it.

Straight Talk

Take some time, perhaps just a few days, and observe yourself in relationship to your kids. Make a mental note of all the ways in which you model healthy relationship dynamics. Ask yourself the tough questions: How often do I accept my child for who she is today and how often do I use a strategy designed to make her change to my liking? Remember, our children are watching and learning, and if they come to believe that healthy relationships include accepting yourself and others, and finding healthy ways to work together to solve problems and overcome challenges, you will be giving them a gift that will last a lifetime.

Message Three – The Truth in Our Words

And finally, let's wrap up this relationship blueprint with examples that illustrate the power of adequately representing the true meaning of the words we use with our kids and the lasting influence they have on our children, now and in their lives as adults.

Respect: If your son is raised connecting the word respect with the following statements:

- "I respect the choice you are making to wear your sandals; I will be wearing my rain boots."
- "I can see how upset you are, and I love you and respect you too much to fight with you, so I am going to go outside until I cool down and then we can talk about what happened."
- "I know you like having the same lunch every day, so I bought you everything you need to make the lunch that you like."
- "I can see that the way you organize your clothes really works for you."
- "I can feel myself getting angry, so I am going to go cool down and think about how I feel about the situation and then maybe we can find a solution that works for all of us."
- "I respect your choice not to work on your science project and I hope you can respect my choice not to get involved in the decision your teacher makes."
- "I know your uncle can be very judgmental and in spite of that, you showed respect for his point of view and for the rest of the family by not arguing with him over dinner."

…it is reasonable that you will raise a son who has a healthy concept of what respect looks like, sounds like, and feels like in a relationship with others.

Message: Respect is a two-way street and we both participate.

Cooperation: If your daughter is raised hearing:

- "How about you carry the jacket to the car just in case the weather changes? If you decide not to wear it, that's fine, but at least you will have it with you."
- "Would you be willing to help me out at the store and be in charge of crossing things off my list and then paying the cashier while I bag the groceries?"
- "I am not going to have time tonight to help you with your project, but if you are willing to get up an hour early tomorrow morning I could help you then."
- "I promised your brother I would make him a cake and I am wondering if you would like me to teach you so we can make our cakes together from now on."
- "I am willing to watch thirty minutes of your show, even though you know it's not my favorite, before I go to the other room to read."
- "We have a lot of camping gear to set up, how do we want to divide up the jobs?"

…it is reasonable that you will raise a daughter who has a healthy concept of what cooperation looks like, sounds like, and feels like in a relationship with others.

Message: Cooperation is a willingness to work together.

Responsibility: If your children are raised hearing:

- "I trust you can find another pair of mittens to wear today at school."
- "Only you can decide how much lunch you will eat."

- "I don't know where you put your soccer shoes. I put mine in the hall closet."
- "I'm sorry, but I won't bring the homework that you left on the counter."
- "You told the coach that you would put in the extra time outside of practice; you'll have to explain to him why that didn't happen."
- "Do you have a plan for replacing the broken window?"
- "I understand that you are frustrated. I am following through with our agreement."

... it is reasonable that you will raise children who have a healthy concept of what responsibility looks like, sounds like, and feels like in a relationship with others.

Message: Responsibility is being able to respond effectively to the situation at hand.

Relationship Recovery

At first this may seem like a lot to digest, but the truth is, every parent I work with starts the conversation by saying, "I don't know what happened to our relationship, but if we don't turn things around, I'm afraid we won't have a relationship at all in a few years," so I know that at the epicenter of the problem is the struggle to engage in healthy relationships with those we love most. As you work your way through the next three chapters, you will begin to see how every step connects and integrates to create a streamlined method for growing a grown-up and enjoying the process along the way.

CHAPTER TWO

Independence Is Imperative

It is imperative that parents come to terms with, and embrace, the inevitable quest for independence and self-reliance that children are destined to take. In my book *Duct Tape Parenting*, I dedicated an entire chapter to this topic and provided parents with strategies and tools to help foster independence in children ages two to twenty-two years.

I encourage parents to accept and acknowledge that the journey toward independence begins as soon as their child takes his first breath and continues each day as the child grows and matures. In fact, if we are honest with ourselves, we know intuitively that we are all striving for full independence and self-reliance, which is what allows us to enter into healthy relationships with members of our family and others. Without a sense of independence and the assurance that we can rely on ourselves, we become dependent on others. This type of codependence puts us at risk as we enter adolescence and can impede our progress as adults. It is our job to help our children construct self-reliance rather than render them dependent on us or on others.

If you aren't convinced of this based on your own experience as an adult and by the dangers of sending ill-prepared children into the adult world, perhaps the expert opinions put forth in Bella English's November 9, 2013, *Boston Globe* article, " 'Snowplow Parents' Overly Involved in College Students' Lives," will help you take fostering independence more seriously; according to the article, "some parents remain so involved that they are leaving their college-age kids anxious, depressed, and ill-equipped to deal with matters both small and large."

In the same article, one expert, Holly Schiffrin, a psychology professor at the University of Mary Washington in Fredericksburg, Virginia, and coauthor of a study, "Helping or Hovering?" published in April 2014 in the *Journal of Child and Family Studies* says, "people need three basic skills to be happy: they need to feel independent, competent, and able to form and maintain relationships with others. Over-involved, 'hover-parenting' interferes with the healthy and appropriate development of these three basic skills."

We've all heard, or perhaps even thought, "Gee, if my three-year-old would only stay this little forever" or "No way is my daughter ever going to be a teenager!" I've seen hundreds of parents use this state of mind (both consciously and unconsciously) to drive their decision making as parents. This nostalgic, idealistic, and wishful thinking overshadows reality. Children are always maturing and asking for more independence. When properly guided, they can handle it. All too often, though, parents don't want their children to grow up. They don't like to admit they are no longer as necessary in their kids' day-to-day lives, so they insert themselves in far too many situations and concern themselves with too many details of their kids' lives. This tendency comes from a good place. But it's just not in the best interest of the child.

We parents may not want to face the truth that children are with us in order to learn how to leave us, but our children understand this truth on a deep and intuitive level. For them, this march toward independence remains at the forefront of their every decision until they have been successfully launched. Unless, of course, a parent convinces the child that independence is something to fear or that she might not be completely prepared for life beyond the threshold of home.

Think about it for just a minute. Our children learn how to roll over, sit up, crawl, and walk without any help from us. They watch our mouths as we talk to them and finally begin to mimic our words, growing more confident each time they are successful. They absorb every word we say and watch the way we respond to their every action. Our children are preparing for the day they leave our homes and strike out on their own, and our job is to support their development, growth, and success.

If we embrace the notion that our children are on a preordained journey toward independence and self-reliance, we can reframe our role in their lives and allow them to be true trailblazers, with the courage and the skills to navigate the adventure we call life and seize all it has to offer. However, we must be ready for things to get messy, to fall apart just a little bit. We must trust that kids can handle more responsibility, learn from failure, and make decisions that might make us weak in the knees but are necessary if they are to continue to mature. No matter how old your children are today, remember that it is never too early or too late to begin fostering their independence.

The Big Picture: Preparing for Departure

So, how are parents supposed to foster independence and ensure their children are self-reliant when they leave home at eighteen? Thankfully, it's simple. By integrating a few easy strategies into daily life with your children, no matter how old they are, you can ensure that they have plenty of time to practice and master the skills necessary to thrive through all stages of life.

The first strategy I recommend parents use is my Timeline for Training assessment tool (you can find this in *Duct Tape Parenting*). This tool allows parents to evaluate their children's current mastery of self, home, social, and life skills. Once parents assess their children's current level of mastery, they are in a position to create a system for teaching their kids all the skills they will need to navigate the world with confidence and enthusiasm.

Beyond teaching such skills, parents can foster independence by providing ample opportunities for their children to make daily choices, participate in family policy discussions, and implement the privilege and responsibility matrix. It requires that, as parents, we remain diligent in our efforts to establish a less-is-more approach that promotes independence in children of all ages.

Where to Start: Create a Timeline for Training

As parents, and as our children's first and most influential teachers, we have eighteen years to prepare our kids to throw open the doors and walk into their lives with confidence. From the moment your children can walk, you can begin to invite them to participate more fully in not only their own lives, but in the life of the family.

The Timeline for Training is a simple tool that you can use to:

• **Assess** your children's competencies in self, home, social, and life skills, so that you can begin fostering their independence without overwhelming them or throwing your family into a state of chaos.

• **Track** the progress and improvement your children are making in the areas of self, home, social, and life skills, so you can support and encourage them. This will inspire them to master new and more difficult skills over time.

• **Identify** the skills your children still need to learn or need more time to master, so they can continue to take on more as they mature and their confidence continues to grow with their level of mastery.

• **Relax** in the confidence that your kids are becoming capable, cooperative, responsible, and respectful individuals who will thrive in their adult lives as a result of your commitment to fostering their independence and creating an environment in which they can become truly self-reliant.

Go Slow: Training Takes Time

Imagine that when your children were very young, they were invited and then trained in basic self and home skills like:

• Choosing their own clothes
• Deciding whether they wanted baths or showers
• Setting an alarm clock and getting up on their own each morning
• Making their own breakfast, lunch, and snacks
• Organizing their own backpacks, homework, and sports equipment

- Setting the table for dinner
- Doing laundry
- Cleaning bathrooms

And you continued to foster their independence when they entered middle school by helping them develop social skills, which included:

- Making phone calls
- Talking with teachers about their grades or homework assignments
- Asking someone out on a date
- Making apologies to people they hurt
- Talking to the bank clerk about their checking account

When they entered high school, you were there to finish your work of helping them master life skills, including:

- Getting a driver's license
- Preparing meals—including planning menus and budgets, shopping, cooking the food, and cleaning up
- Maintaining the home
- Helping with financial activities
- Locating and securing resources (doctors, insurance, and so on)

And you didn't shirk the scary areas of parenting, including:

- Navigating drugs and drinking
- Participating in healthy sexual relationships (or not)
- Heading off to college
- Other risky decisions young adults are faced with

How do you think life in your family would be affected if you were committed to helping your children become more independent and self-reliant with each year? How would this change the relationship you have with your children now? What values and character traits would you be supporting and encouraging? And finally, how do you think your children will fare as young adults, navigating life on their own after years of practice?

Using the Timeline for Training to foster independence and self-reliance in our kids ensures that we are adequately preparing them for the challenges of adult life and at the same time guarantees that life at home will be more joyful and pleasant.

Be Ready: What If My Child Resists?

Your children may be resistant to you teaching them how to do more for themselves and for the family because they have always had, and quite enjoy, the "maid service." It doesn't matter whether they are resistant or not. We know as parents that there's nothing worse than sending an eighteen-year-old out into the world unprepared, and none of us would do it intentionally. So you will have to muster up the courage to move past their resistance without taking it personally or resorting to ineffective strategies to force them to help out. Otherwise, you will be faced with throwing in the towel and going back to doing everything yourself. Some of your children's resistance might be due to the fact that they feel like they can't do the job right or that they will be corrected repeatedly if they try. Be sure to encourage your children to do their best, and fight the temptation to point out their mistakes.

Stay Focused: Age-Appropriate Skills

Following is a partial list of the self, home, social, and life skills you can begin teaching your children from the time they are very young. As I like to say, "If they can walk, they can work." They will thank you for this eventually, because we all know that "work is worth."

Remember that children are different and they progress at their own pace, so resist the urge to compare or criticize. Remember, everyone is practicing, and that includes you.

Birth to Age Nine: Focus on Self Skills and Home Skills

Believe it or not, children are eager both to learn how to do things for themselves and to help their family out. And they need no outside motivation from a parent or anyone else.

What every child needs is an invitation from a parent to participate fully in life, and that starts with teaching kids how to take care of themselves and then extending that invitation until they are helping with family life.

Before long, your children will be an integral part of the success of the family, their sense of independence will grow, and they will feel more and more capable as they learn and then master new skills.

- Making bed
- Brushing teeth
- Taking shower/bath
- Washing hair
- Getting dressed
- Making breakfast/lunch
- Packing backpack
- Remembering sports stuff
- Organizing homework

- Setting table
- Unloading dishwasher
- Cleaning the bathroom
- Vacuuming
- Making grocery list
- Learning how to cook
- Doing laundry
- Stacking wood

Ages Ten to Fifteen: Focus on Social Skills

This is possibly the most challenging time to decide that your kids should "step up" and "take responsibility" for self and home skills for two reasons. First, remember that you are the one who assigned yourself the role as the maid, not the kids. In all likelihood your kids *cannot* do what you do because they haven't been taught how to do these tasks or been given a chance to practice the skill until they mastered it.

Second, kids are supposed to be learning social skills that will define them as individuals and as a generation. Parents who are still treating teens like seven-year-olds, nagging them about clean rooms and showers, are interfering with their development. The opportunity to develop healthy social skills fosters independence.

- Making phone calls
- Asking someone out
- Breaking up with someone she no longer wants to date
- Telling a friend he is worried about his friend's safety
- Making apologies to people he hurts
- Talking to the bank clerk about his checking account
- Standing up for kids who are being picked on
- Balancing responsibilities and technology
- Talking with teachers about her grades or homework assignments

Ages Sixteen to Eighteen:
Life Skills and Identifying Values

Our children are getting ready for life beyond our threshold. They know that they are leaving. The question is, will they be ready?

- Opening bank accounts
- Making doctors' appointments
- Buying insurance
- Going to college
- Moving out
- Managing schedules
- Dating
- Driving
- Drinking
- Drugs
- Stealing
- Cheating

Imagine that your children felt confident about their abilities to manage their lives, looked forward to growing up, felt supported and encouraged by their parents, had plenty of practice, made lots of mistakes and learned from them, and trusted you because you trusted them.

A Balancing Act: Privileges and Responsibilities

Before discussing privileges and responsibilities, it's important to define the two. **Privileges are the things our kids want:**

- Later bedtimes
- Meals out
- Sports participation
- Sleepovers
- Outings to the movies
- The newest devices
- Access to technology
- Dating
- Driving
- Later curfews

Responsibilities are the "to-do" items that accompany the privilege; a child must convince his parents he can handle the accompanying responsibilities before his parents say yes to the new privilege:

- Going to bed without a fight and without a thirty-minute bedtime routine
- Getting up by himself
- Handling her morning
- Keeping her hands to herself
- Cleaning up the kitchen after he has made a snack
- Sitting at the table with the rest of the family, using good manners
- Performing his daily contribution without pushback
- Managing her time and her stuff
- Respecting family policies like curfews
- Getting and holding down a job

As children grow and mature, they will naturally want to do more and more on their own, with their friends, and out in the larger world. It is essential to remember that with each privilege, comes a certain responsibility. As they ask for more, it is our job to say yes, as long as they show they can handle the responsibilities that go with their requests.

Here's what this system looks like:

Privilege: Eating out
Responsibilities:

- Practice table manners
- Eat what you order
- Sit still in your seat
- Engage in conversation
- Make eye contact
- Say please and thank you
- Maintain a respectful tone of voice

Privilege: No naps/staying up late
Responsibilities:

- Wake up in the morning on time
- Find something quiet to do so other family members can rest or sleep
- Follow through with daily contributions
- Follow through with agreements
- Maintain respect for yourself and family members
- Stay awake in school or during other daily events
- Maintain manners and common courtesies

Privilege: Visiting at a friend's house
Responsibilities:

- Demonstrate cooperation with your own family members (this lets you know your child can cooperate with others)
- Show respect for yourself and family members (no physical or verbal aggression)
- Follow through with agreements
- Practice manners and common courtesies
- Call if plans change
- Demonstrate problem-solving without yelling or hitting someone

Privilege: Borrowing the family car
Responsibilities:

- Be employed gainfully
- Replace the gas you used
- Return on time
- Contribute toward insurance, car maintenance, and so on

- Uphold family policies, i.e., no drinking and driving, no texting and driving etc. Come home sober.

Privilege: Using the computer
Responsibilities:

- Follow through with agreements
- Manage time

- Finish homework
- View appropriate content
- Complete contributions

Remember:

- Age five years and younger: give children seven days to prove they are responsible
- Age five to nine years: give children seven to ten days

- Age nine years and older: give children thirty days

Privileges and Responsibilities Foster Independence

Here are a few examples to illustrate how you can use Privileges and Responsibilities to foster independence no matter the age or developmental stage of your child.

Your four-year-old won't sit still at the table. He is up and down, plays with his food, climbs on your lap, and demands his favorite pasta instead of the chicken you have already prepared for the family. You may argue, lecture, give in, or punish him in an attempt to teach him proper table manners. In spite of your bribes and threats, there is no indication that your child can sit through a meal and demonstrate even rudimentary manners; however, you continue to take him out to eat, where he displays the same behavior that you see at home. Eating out, whether it is at your parents' house or at a five-star restaurant, is a privilege, and the age-appropriate responsibilities that go along with that include sitting in your seat, speaking in a quiet voice, and using the utensils supplied by the restaurant. Balancing privileges with responsibilities fosters independence and self-reliance in our children.

Your seven-year-old wants a later bedtime, but the current nighttime routine is a horror show. You have to nag him to go upstairs, brush his teeth, and put on his pajamas. He whines, runs around the house, and teases the dog until you threaten that you won't read him a book unless he goes upstairs immediately. Although he hightails it upstairs, he proceeds to mess around in the bathroom and jump on the bed, and he can't manage to pick out a book. A bedtime routine that should take ten minutes often takes thirty minutes or more. Your son continues to badger you about a later bedtime, so you make some half-hearted agreements and give it a go. It goes exactly the way it has always gone. A later bedtime is a privilege, and the age-appropriate responsibilities that go along with that include taking care of your own personal hygiene, putting yourself to sleep, and navigating your responsibilities the next day with ease and adequate energy.

Your nine-year-old has begged you for his own cell phone, and although you don't think it's a good idea, he has worn you down. You purchase the phone, give a lecture regarding the rules and use of the phone, and the fighting begins. He does all the things you might expect of an inexperienced nine-year-old who has not been shown the connection between the privilege of having a phone and the responsibilities that go along with it. Hence, he frequently leaves it at school or the ball field, forcing you to make extra trips (which, by the way, is another missed opportunity to help him become more independent). He may drop it so often that it breaks; because he has no job, you lecture him about being careful and you replace it. Your opportunity to foster his independence is lost, because you felt obligated or pressured to provide him with the latest technology.

Your sixteen-year-old wants a car and you consider getting her one. Her grades are good, she has a good group of friends, and she is still speaking to you in a civil tone, unlike many others her age. What she doesn't have is a job, and she has not been the most responsible kid when it comes to pulling her weight in the family or respecting other people's property (she borrows clothes without returning them). Against your better judgment you decide to buy her the car anyway, and within weeks you notice a few things that give you concern. First, you are paying not only for her gas and her insurance but for the upkeep of the car as well. Second, now that she can drive herself, she asks for a little pocket change so she can go and get herself a "latte" because she is "dragging" or Chinese takeout for her study group. Suddenly, her car is costing you extra money. Third, she has broken curfew on a number of occasions, along with other family policies, and seems unconcerned when you threaten to take the car away. You realize you are spending more time fighting with your daughter now than you have at any other time in your relationship. Her opportunities to become more independent are being ripped away from her, because you have provided her with a privilege without allowing her the opportunity to master the accompanying responsibilities.

In each of these scenarios parents have the chance to foster their child's independence by asking the child to consistently accept the responsibilities that go along with each privilege. Each time a privilege is given without identifying the required responsibilities and allowing the child to practice them outside your home, your child loses another opportunity to become independent.

Reality Check: This System Matters

I've never heard of a utility company waiving a bill for a nineteen-year-old who wanted a new snowboard or the landlord looking the other way when a twentysomething just had to have the latest bag in the department store window. Even if we don't take the time to teach our kids about the balance between privileges and responsibilities, the world certainly will. It's easy to see that if we miss these golden moments that teach them, their ability to become independent is compromised; and when the world teaches them, the consequences are typically less forgiving.

By using the Privileges and Responsibilities strategy, you can alleviate power struggles and avoid raising children who feel entitled to the privileges of life. Parents who do not employ this strategy run the risk of raising children who enter adulthood completely unprepared for the responsibilities and demands that life will place on them. Remember, it is our job to adequately represent to our children what they can expect from the outside world. This is love. This is respect.

Unfortunately, society tends to make us feel obliged to provide children with nonstop, ever-evolving privileges (including technology, activities, camps, new clothing, and so on), despite the fact that our children do not, without training, have the skills to handle all these privileges. Too often, parents cave to this pressure. When we do this out of a sense of guilt, pressure from our friends, or a desire for prestige it severely disrupts our children's ability to become independent, self-reliant, and responsible people.

Straight Talk

The following is a list of points to remember:

- Your job is to say YES to your child's request for more independence in the form of privileges.
- Your child's job is to CONVINCE you that it is a good idea for you to say YES to his request by showing you that he understands and can live up to the responsibilities associated with the privilege.
- This balance is what helps set up a healthy, mutually respectful relationship where the child is given an opportunity to prove that she is "growing into" a responsible adult. This will keep parents from giving too much or withholding too much.
- Under no circumstances believe a promise. Instead, follow this motto: Don't listen to the mouth, watch the feet.
- Allow for seven, twenty-one, or thirty days of consistency before you say YES again.

- By using privileges and responsibilities effectively, you will limit the number of power struggles and disagreements, and the confusion by as much as 80 percent.
- Do not use this strategy as a form of punishment or bribery. This is not a tool to hold over your children's heads to get them to do what you want.

Stay Steady: Words to Live By

"Say what you mean, mean what you say ... then do it."
It might be hard to see how this simple statement could help foster independence in your kids, but I'm confident that if you incorporate this phrase into daily life with children, you will be amazed at the results. When your kids ask the second or third (or fourth) time and you stick to your resolve, they will, eventually, stop asking a second or third (or fourth) time. But they will not stop until they are sure that when you say something, you mean it and you will do it. This is a two-way street. When your kids don't mean what they say ("I'll clean my room before I go to Klara's") and you hold up your end of the bargain ("I'll take you to Klara's as soon as you clean the room"), you will see their behavior change. Not only are you modeling what it looks like to be trusted, you are helping your child hold herself accountable.

Here is what I typically observe when I work with parents who are struggling with this concept:

"Maggie, we can go to the park as soon as you put all the stuffed animals back in your toy box." Ten minutes later, stuffed animals still on the floor or picked up by mom, Maggie is putting her coat on and heading to the park.

"Charles, there is no dessert unless you clear all your dishes from the table." Charles takes his plate but leaves the rest, and delights in the cupcakes served to him for dessert.

"Charlotte, you are not going to Cindy's until you pick up all the supplies from your science project." After a weak attempt at picking up, with supplies still littering the table, Charlotte is headed to Cindy's.

"Malcolm, I am not driving you to the tournament until you clean up your room and put the laundry I washed for you away." Malcolm pushes both clean and dirty clothes to the side, brings four plates encrusted with food down to the kitchen, which is about 10 percent of what needs to happen to constitute a clean room, and he is transported to the tournament seventy miles away.

Each time a parent makes a request or a contingency and does not follow through, he undermines the child's chance to become more independent and self-sufficient. It also damages the relationship between parent and child. Think back to the previous chapter. How might these daily interactions affect the child's relationship blueprint?

When you can finally embrace this motto and embed it into your parenting approach, you are able to manage your tendency to say one thing—" We are not going to the park until you pick up all the blocks"—and then do another—give in, because it's easier. When you follow through, you create the space for your child to develop the courage and the skills she needs to thrive as an adult.

Invite Kids to Think: Essential Practice for Adulthood

By inviting our children into the decision-making process from the earliest age, we are giving them the opportunity to grow into independent, self-reliant, and thoughtful adults.

Choices: We can begin fostering independence in our very young children by offering them choices on a regular basis. Choices are not ultimatums with a perceived correct answer: "You can put your shoes on right now or I am carrying you to the car." Choices are win–win situations: "Would you like to walk to the car barefoot and carry your shoes or would you like to put your shoes on and hold my hand while we walk to the car?" "Would you like to wear your shoes or your boots?" "Would you like to walk or run?" "Would you like to hold my left hand or right hand?"

Offering a young child limited choices:

1. Alleviates many of the power struggles that start when a parent gives a directive to a child: "Please go get dressed." Offering a choice equalizes power, fosters independence, and invites the child to participate more fully in something that will affect him directly: "Would you like to get dressed now or after you eat breakfast?"

2. Implies that the parent, adult, or authority figure has some level of faith that the child can make a reasonable choice. If this message is conveyed consistently over the course of many months, the child begins to view herself as a capable person who can figure out reasonable choices before they are offered. This in and of itself fosters a sense of independence: "I don't need my parent to offer me a choice. I can figure out the options all by myself."

3. Provides the child the opportunity to make thoughtful, reasonable choices with positive outcomes as well as choices with negative outcomes. Over time, this experience contributes greatly to a child's sense that he is prepared to take on more responsibility for his life with the skills necessary to navigate the world beyond his home.

4. Teaches children that choosing not to choose is in itself a choice. The only remedy is for someone else to make the choice for the child. If you offer a child a choice and she refuses to choose, then you are forced to choose. This is about all the motivation a child needs to take on the job of making choices, which further fosters independence.

Decision making: As children graduate from simple choices to the individual act of on-the-spot decision making in new areas of life, they are offered opportunities to develop new levels of independence: "There is no one here to give me a choice and I have never been in this situation before. I could do a, b, or c. What decision will I make for myself?" We can certainly see how this enriches the child's confidence in his abilities and further fosters the idea that he has what it takes to make his way in the world. Children who are confident in their ability to make choices and rebound from choices that did not turn out very well have the confidence required to make a decision and move forward. These children know that even good decision-makers sometimes make mistakes, but if they make a mistake, they have what it takes to move through it. Perhaps at no other time in a child's life will he feel the full weight and sheer joy of making an independent decision. This is true empowerment; nobody else is to blame if it goes badly and nobody else can take credit if it goes well.

The more practice children are afforded to make decisions and experience both the positive and negative outcomes of those decisions, the better they understand their abilities. Allowing a child, whenever possible, to make decisions without input from a parent, adult, or authority figure furthers the child's independent nature and increases the confidence he has in his own abilities.

Initiating policies: Once our children graduate from the process of making simple choices and then master making independent decisions, their natural progression is toward applying their expertise with the entire family. Years of practice making choices and decisions prepare children to engage in a more dynamic and robust conversation with parents, adults, and authority figures as equal partners in designing family policy. Family policy is set around areas of curfew, dating, parties, alcohol, drugs, driving, and even the basic contributions. Children who understand their influence on the policy for everyone in the family develop a strong sense of belonging. These kids will do little to upset that connection and foundational bond.

From choices to decisions to establishing policy, it's clear that the parents' role is to foster independence in children of all ages and ensure that when they leave home at eighteen, they have both the skills and the experience necessary to keep them on a trajectory of independence and self-reliance.

CHAPTER THREE

Living with a Toddler, Raising an Adult

As parents, most of us understand on some level that our primary responsibility is to ensure that our children grow up under our roof and eventually leave to enter adulthood at eighteen years of age. We know they should be ready to make a positive contribution to their community, have the skills necessary to navigate the world successfully, and possess the character traits critical to creating a satisfying and fulfilling life. Although we know this, it can be hard to articulate and identify exactly how we're going to pull this off. Our visions of parenting get clouded when we are forced to cohabitate with people (our children) we sometimes don't understand. Life isn't always easy.

Daydreams Versus Reality

We've all daydreamed about snuggling with our newborn babes, living with toddlers who shower us with hugs and kisses, and embracing first days of school, skinned knees, soccer games, sleepovers, and family vacations. We've envisioned raising kids who turn into happy, confident, secure, resilient, responsible, compassionate, and hardworking adults. We hope, and in some cases pray, that one day our adult children will confirm for us that we nailed it as their parents. We want to remain connected to our children throughout their childhood, create positive memories with them, and look forward to welcoming our adult children home for frequent visits. This is the dream most of us share. Still, as most parents discover, it isn't long before the challenges of living with a young child with an emerging personality take over and all idyllic thoughts of raising a superbly adjusted, non-jerk, kickass, compassionate, kind, and resilient human are sidelined

We discover the realities don't match the visions and we think, *Someday we'll get back to raising the competent adult… but right now, let me put out this parenting fire.*

My First Big Aha Parenting Moment

Although I couldn't have articulated my thoughts at the time, as a young mother I could sense that my job went well beyond figuring out feeding and sleeping schedules and teaching my daughter how to pour her own juice or tie her shoes. I sensed that, although this was what daily life would look like for many years, I was on a bigger mission. This big idea—the challenge of managing daily life with kids while keeping my eye on raising an awesome adult—was a clear reality that hit me one day as I found myself juggling two young, demanding children with different needs, schedules, moods, and personalities. I realized that I was making the kinds of parenting decisions that had nothing to do with raising a happy, healthy future adult. I was focusing only on the here and now. I was parenting a moody four-year-old, not a future twenty-four-year-old.

Like so many parents, I had lost sight of what was happening beyond the moment. I became depressed and unenthusiastic when it hit me that my entire parenting career was going to be summarized as "expert bottom wiper and snack fetcher." This was discouraging and frustrating. I called a good-humored friend and colleague whom I knew would understand my situation. I was looking for encouragement, empathy, I wasn't sure what, but I needed some fresh thinking on the situation.

As I told my friend about my "parenting life crisis," she said quite simply and with confident experience, "Vicki, you are trying to reconcile living with a toddler, while raising an adult." Although the power of those words didn't sink in initially, I knew that I was having an "aha" moment. I remember thinking that what I'd just heard was going to change the way I parented my kids. In the moment, however, I remember thinking to myself, *Raising an adult? Who is she kidding? I will be lucky if I get them off to kindergarten in one piece.*

Later that night, as I was mulling over what my friend had said, I realized that what I had been struggling with was indeed my desire to reconcile in my own mind the challenge of living with a toddler while raising a future adult. I knew all the best intentions could be derailed by the realities of raising a busy two-year-old, a fussy three-year-old, a mercurial four-year-old, and so on. I knew this was going to be my biggest challenge: making decisions every day that would keep my long-term goal of raising a healthy adult in the forefront. I also realized that this would be my greatest and most rewarding parenting objective. And so I set out to learn as much as I could about raising children into successful adulthood—in other words, how to grow a grown-up.

I have never, in all my years working with parents, heard one of them say, "I really look forward to diving into the next book, blog, article, or podcast to learn how to deal with yet another pesky behavioral problem." And happily I can introduce parents to the one and only concept I used in dealing with each and every pesky, annoying, hair-pulling behavioral challenge any one of my five kids threw my way during our lives together.

The Four Mistaken Goals of Behavior (The Only Strategy You'll Ever Need)

One of the greatest life gifts I ever received was the introduction to the work of Dr. Rudolph Dreikurs and his genius strategy for dealing with any and all child behaviors; this includes biting, spitting, hitting, and throwing toys. It also offers solutions for naptime and bedtime,

Straight Talk

"The misbehaving child is still trying in a mistaken way to feel important in his world. A young child who has never been allowed to dress himself, because his mother is always in a hurry or has to make sure all of his clothes match; or who has not been allowed

> to help in the house because he cannot do it as well, will lack the feeling that he is a useful, contributing member of the family, and will feel important only when arousing his parent's anger and annoyance with his misbehavior. The child is usually unaware of his goals. His behavior, though illogical to others, is consistent with his own interpretation of his place in the family group." (The ABC's of Guiding the Child, *Dreikurs and Goldman 3-4*)

brushing hair or teeth, bathing, eating, and listening. If a parent were to try to address every single one of these challenges individually, it would require hours and hours of personal research and testing. His four mistaken goals of behavior form a straightforward philosophy with accompanying strategies that addresses the plethora of unique challenges that come with raising young kids. I have found this to be a supremely foolproof and accessible approach that any parent in any context can rely on when attempting to problem solve in the moment (while keeping an eye on the future).

When Life Intrudes on Best Laid Plans

But let's get real for a minute: the question becomes, *Yeah...how do I reconcile living with a toddler while raising an adult when my kid is tossing broccoli across the kitchen?* Or *Sure, I'll be mutually respectful except my kid won't listen to a word I say.*

As parents, we can feel increasingly compelled to "make the bad behaviors stop" or "get kids to do what we want," which is completely understandable if we have only the short-term goal of parenting in mind, but this "feed the weed" thinking begets more misbehavior and, consequently, more frustration. There are hundreds, if not thousands, of behaviors that drive parents crazy and, more importantly, don't serve our children in the long term. The trick is in how we deal with them—all of them—and not lose our minds in the process. The Four Mistaken Goals of Behavior offer the answer to our prayers.

From Toddler to Teenager

Here's how the four mistaken goals of behavior work, in a nutshell. Every child behaves in a way that serves his immediate purpose. The purpose is one of the following:

- I want your **attention.**
- I want more **power.**
- I feel hurt and want to **hurt** you back.
- I don't think I have what it takes to deal with this situation so I will **avoid** it.

Sometimes you will see the same pesky behavior, such as refusing to sit at the table, teasing a sibling, or leaving toys around the house, in one or more of your kids, but for two completely different reasons. This is where Dreikurs's theory and accompanying strategies consider the uniqueness of each family dynamic. Identifying the behavior or challenge isn't nearly as important as understanding the purpose of the misbehavior. So, in short, the behavior is secondary. It doesn't matter what form the nonsense your child is throwing your way takes, what matters is understanding the purpose of the behavior. Because there are only four options to choose from, it's like winning the parenting lottery.

The next, not-so-obvious question is, if a child who is throwing food could be doing so for one of these four reasons, how do I know which one it is? Easy—your feelings tell you what the goal is.

Attention: No matter what the behavior is, you feel frustrated, annoyed, and exhausted.

Power: No matter what the behavior is, you feel angry, provoked, challenged, or threatened.

Revenge: No matter what the behavior is, you feel hurt, personally insulted, or disappointed.

Avoidance: No matter what the behavior is, you feel like throwing in the towel. You have tried everything and nothing works. You feel hopeless and helpless.

Parenting Solutions

Remember, working on repairing the relationship and helping your kids become more independent is a project for the long haul, but there is still the question of what to do in the moment. As parents, we want to know what to do in the middle of a meltdown, tantrum, or full-on power struggle. Before you do anything though, remember these tips:

- No matter the pesky behavior your child throws your way, it is for one of only four reasons.
- To determine the reason, use your feelings to quickly and accurately determine the child's goal.
- At the epicenter of all pesky behavior is a fractured relationship, a lack of training (which leads to overdependent children), or both.
- You learned in chapters 1 and 2 how to go about creating a healthy relationship with your kids and how to foster their independence; it won't be long before you see real change in the way your children behave and the way the family functions.

There are two things to keep in mind when you find yourself in the red zone moment: first, don't make things worse, and second, move the action forward until you are all calm and you can refocus your efforts on repairing or improving the relationship and fostering independence. In the moment, however, you have lots of options to choose from, and here is just a sample of what's available:

- **Ignore the behavior.** You can still be kind to your child and ignore her demands, cries, or interruptions (as long as you are sure she is not in any real physical distress).

- **Encourage your child** (a misbehaving child is a discouraged child): "I know it's *hard, frustrating, tiring…*" or "I'll give you some

> ## Straight Talk
>
> When you find yourself in the red zone, remember, there are two criteria:
>
> - Don't make things worse
> - Move the action forward
>
> This is not, I repeat *not*, a teachable moment. This is a moment for you to make an observation and use the information you gather to make an informed parenting decision when you are calm and thoughtful.

privacy to work it out and if you are still struggling come and find me" or "Show me what you can do."

- **Refuse to get into a power struggle.** This means having the self-control to walk away and cool down. Remember, you are a role model for the behavior you want to see your kids demonstrate.

- **Act, don't talk.** That may mean removing the plate from the table if the child gets up repeatedly or taking the toy truck and putting it away if it's being used as a rocket launcher or walking into the bedroom and closing the door if your child is trying to hit, pinch, or bite you. Actions get children's attention; words put them to sleep.

- **Give a choice.** "Would you like to use a mop or a rag to clean up the mess?"

Breaking Down the Four Goals of Mistaken Behavior

Following is a comprehensive list for you to use until this simple strategy becomes second nature, and I promise you, within a few short weeks this process will seem effortless to you. This is a tool commonly used by Adlerian parent educators, and not my own creation. You can download a copy of this chart at vickihoefle.com or you can visit any one of the websites associated with alfredadler.org and find a similar version of the information.

Child's Mistaken Goal: Attention

The child believes: I only count when I'm being noticed
    The child feels: Insecure, alienated
    The adult feels: Irritated, annoyed, exhausted
    Strategies used to deal with behavior:

- Reminding
- Nagging
- Coaxing
- Doing things for the child
- Talking-talking-talking
- Telling them to find something to do

What usually happens: The child stops temporarily but later resumes the same or another attention-getting behavior
    What the child is really saying: Include me, involve me, invite me
    What adults can do to encourage useful behavior:

- Say something only once, then act
- Plan special time
- Set up routines
- Take time for training
- Have family meetings
- Touch without words
- Redirect by involving child in a useful task, so he gets positive attention
- Say what you will do: *"I love you and ..."*; *"I can paint with you as soon as I finish what I am doing"*
- Avoid special services

- Have faith in the child's ability to deal with her feelings
- Do not try to make things better or fix the situation

Child's new belief: I belong
Child's feeling: Secure
Child's *new* goal: Cooperation

Child's Mistaken Goal: Power

The child believes: I belong only when I am the boss or in control, or when I am proving no one can boss me: "You can't make me and you can't stop me."
    The child feels: Inadequate, dependent, others are in control
    The adult feels: Angry, provoked, challenged, threatened
    Strategies used to deal with behavior:

- Proving the child can't get away with his misbehavior
- Insisting he do what he is told
- Fighting
- Giving in

What usually happens: Misbehavior intensifies and power struggles increase
    What the child is really saying: Show me, teach me, let me help, give me choices
    What adults can do to encourage useful behavior:

- Acknowledge that you can't make the child do something, and ask for help
- Offer a limited choice
- Redirect
- Do not fight and do not give in
- Withdraw from conflict and calm down
- Be firm and kind
- Act, don't talk

- Decide what you will do
- Let routines be the boss
- Develop mutual respect
- Follow through

Child's new belief: I can do it
    Child's feelings: Competent and in control of self
    Child's *new* goal: Self-reliance

Child's Mistaken Goal: Revenge

The child believes: You are against me; nobody really likes me; I'll show you how it feels; I will get back or I will get even
    The child feels: Insignificant
    The adult feels: Hurt, disappointed
    Strategies used to deal with behavior:

- Punishing
- Asking, "How could you do this to me? us? them?"
- Communicating disappointment or hurt feelings
- Teaching the child a lesson

    What usually happens: The child tries to get even, behaves in more destructive ways to make herself unlikeable
    What the child is really saying: Help me, love me, accept me
    What adults can do to encourage useful behavior:

- Deal with the hurt feelings: "Your behavior tells me you must feel hurt. Can we talk about that?"
- Don't take behavior personally
- Avoid punishment and retaliation
- Build trust
- Apologize
- Make amends
- Show you care
- Act, don't talk

- Encourage strengths
- Use family meetings

Child's new belief: I matter
Child's feelings: Significant and valued
Child's *new* goal: Making a contribution

Child's Mistaken Goal: Avoidance

The child believes: I don't believe I can, so I will convince others not to expect anything of me; I can't do anything right so I won't try, and my failures won't be so obvious
The child feels: Inferior, useless, hopeless
The adult feels: Despairing, hopeless, and helpless
Strategies used to deal with behavior:

- Quitting or giving up
- Throwing in the towel
- Rescuing the child
- Making excuses for the child

What usually happens: The child remains passive, there is little or no change, the child becomes more hopeless and displays more inadequacies
What the child is really saying: Have faith in me, don't give up on me!
What adults can do to encourage useful behavior:

- Build on interests
- Use family meetings
- Take time for training
- Take small steps
- Make the task easier until the child experiences success
- Show faith in the child's ability
- Break task down to small steps
- Set up opportunities for success

- Teach skills/show how, but don't do for
- Stop all criticism
- Encourage any positive attempt, no matter how small
- Focus on strengths
- Don't pity
- Don't give up
- Enjoy the child

Child's new belief: I can handle what comes; I feel hopeful and I am willing to try
   Child's feelings: Significant, valuable
   Child's *new* goal: Resilience

Practice Identifying the Mistaken Goal

Let's walk through four scenarios that show a child misbehaving and uncover the goal of each behavior. Remember, the child's goal is identified by the parent's feeling. Each mistaken goal could be different depending upon the child, the parent, and the relationship.

Parent: "My three-year-old keeps shoving her plate off of the table and making a mess. Then she whines and wants me to pick it up for her. If I ask her to clean it up before I get her more, she refuses unless I get down and help her. I am so frustrated with her."

Parent: "My five-year-old is impossible these days. He is constantly teasing his brother and the dog, refusing to do anything I ask him to do unless I help him. I find myself getting increasingly angry at him as the day goes on."

Parent: "My seven-year-old has begun acting out at school. The teacher is very concerned, and when I try and talk to my daughter she covers her ears and runs away or says she hates school and will not go. I need to know what's going on so I can help her but I don't know how to get her to talk to me."

Parent: "My ten-year-old refuses to get himself up in the morning, even though he can and has for several years. He refuses to do his homework and it doesn't matter what I try, he turns it into a fight, stomps away, calls me names, and then slams the door. I can't just let him sleep in or not make him do his homework. I have no idea what to do."

Step one: Identify the behavior that you find troubling and write it down as if you were a scientist or objective observer.

- Three-year-old keeps **pushing her dish** off the table.
- Five-year-old is **teasing and refusing** to help mom.
- Seven-year-old is acting out at school and **refuses to talk with mom and dad** about what is going on.
- Ten-year-old is **refusing to take care** of himself or **do his homework,** and is lashing out at mom and dad.

Step two: Identify how you *feel* about what is happening.

- I am **annoyed and frustrated** when I see the plate fly off of the table (you could just as easily feel angry or disappointed).
- I am **angry** when my child teases and refuses to help me (you could just as easily feel annoyed or hopeless).
- I am **disappointed** in my daughter when I hear she is acting out and I am hurt when she won't talk to me about what is going on (you could just as easily feel annoyed or angry).
- I feel **helpless** when my ten-year-old acts like he can't take care of himself and then lashes out at me (you could just as easily feel angry, annoyed, or disappointed).

Step three: Identify how you generally *react* to the behavior (it's being fueled by your feelings).

- I start **nagging and lecturing** my three-year-old and try to get her to stop throwing the dish on the floor.
- I **yell** at my five-year-old and **punish** him if he keeps refusing to help.

- I try to show my child just how hurtful her behavior is **by hurting her** in some small way, like **throwing all her Legos away**.
- I find myself just **giving up**, throwing in the towel, and walking away.

Step four: Based on your feelings and confirmed by your actions, deduce what the mistaken behavior could be:

- My three-year-old is looking for my undivided **attention.**
- My five-year-old is seeking **power.**
- My seven-year-old is using **revenge** because she feels hurt.
- My ten-year-old is looking for ways to **avoid** anything he thinks he won't be good at.

We're All Raising Future Adults

If we want our adult children to live rich and satisfying lives, with wonderful jobs, great friends, and strong connections to family, we are going to have to help them develop character traits that will assist them in all of these areas.

I know how difficult it is to remember your future twenty-six-year-old when your six-year-old is refusing to do his homework or screaming at you for forgetting his soccer shoes, but the fact remains that it is our job to remember in these moments that we are responsible for helping our children develop character traits that will ensure a healthy adult life.

It goes without saying that there are numerous character traits we want to foster in our children, and I encourage you to make your own list and incorporate it into your parenting. For the purposes of this book, it's more important that you understand how to incorporate this element into the method than it is to identify every character trait you hope your children will embody as adults. Here is a list of adjectives I have compiled over the years. Use it to inspire you to bring the element into daily life with your kids.

Accepting	Encouraging	Resourceful
Appreciative	Flexible	Respectful of
Available	Forgiving	others
Balanced	Generous	Respectful of self
Compassionate	Grateful	Responsible
Confident	Happy	Secure
Connected	Hardworking	Self-Controlled
Content	Humble	Self-Disciplined
Courageous	Humorous	Self-Regulated
Creative	Inquisitive	Sensitive
Curious	Joyful	Sincere
Decisive	Kind	Steadfast
Dependable	Loyal	Tenacious
Determined	Motivated	Thoughtful
Diligent	Patient	Tolerant
Enthusiastic	Peaceful	Welcoming
Empathetic	Resilient	

Character Traits Calm a Powerful Personality

Here is a story about Marianne and her parents, who identified character traits that would help their daughter deal more effectively with day-to-day frustrations and challenges and assist her in her life as an adult.

Background: seven-year-old Marianne is a notoriously precocious child. Her parents, John and Amy, describe her as daring, fearless, mercurial, and intense. Over the years, John and Amy have tried any number of parenting strategies to deal with their daughter's tantrums, emotional breakdowns, overbearing nature, and unpredictable mood changes. "When she was young we tried reasoning with her and giving her choices. Over time, we realized that we were giving in to her demands as a way to avoid her meltdowns and volatile nature. When we realized things were getting worse, we brought down the hammer. We used time-outs, naughty chairs, and taking things away from her, and for a while this seemed to work. We felt like we were getting the upper hand. Unfortunately, getting the upper hand meant that we were losing the dynamic little girl that we often bragged about behind closed doors. John would often say, after a particularly trying day, 'We aren't raising a wimp, that's for sure.' So we started to ease up again and went back to reasoning, giving her choices, and trying to make agreements with her, but so far, nothing has worked for more than an instant or perhaps a day or two."

Situation: on Friday afternoon Marianne was scheduled to attend a reunion of school friends who had moved and were attending a different school. She was excited about the reunion and her behavior started to escalate on the drive to meet her friends. Amy and John told Marianne that if she didn't calm down, they would pull the car over and, depending on how fast she could "pull it together," would keep going or turn around and go home. She calmed down for a few minutes, but it wasn't long before she started to escalate again. John and Amy gave Marianne another warning and then another, then made a threat, and then Amy turned around and yelled at Marianne to "Knock it off!" These exchanges continued until they arrived at the gathering, where Marianne burst out of the car, ran to her friends, and her escalating behavior reached the red zone within minutes. All Amy and John wanted to do was get their daughter out of there and back home.

> **Note from Vicki:** This example shows clearly how dealing with the situation in the moment with no clear plan didn't lead to temporary success, let alone a long-term solution for handling Marianne's high-intensity personality and behaviors. It's clear that if Amy and John continue to deal with Marianne in the same way, they will all suffer years of power struggles.

Now let's add character traits that John and Amy believe are necessary for living a healthy, independent adult life and see if they will have any influence on daily life with their precocious daughter. John and Amy identified self-control, contentment, and resilience as key to their own sense of satisfaction and success as adults, but they never considered fostering these qualities in their young daughter. Here is their account of how things changed with Marianne once they began focusing on these qualities in their day-to-day interactions with her.

We started with contentment and realized that we spent hours with Marianne flip-flopping our roles between parent and playmate. She was so accustomed to having our attention that it was almost impossible for her to spend any time alone. We realized that if she couldn't engage us by asking us to play a game with her or read her a book that her behavior would escalate into an almost frantic state. She would start racing around the house and jumping on furniture until she got our attention, and then the destructive dynamic would begin. We decided that every evening we would sit together in the front room, set the timer for ten minutes, and do something by ourselves quietly, but still be in the same room. Slowly we increased the time and then we began to spend time in different rooms with the timer set. I know it sounds crazy, but she was like a different child. Instead of running around the kitchen trying to get my attention when I was cooking she started to read quietly in the kitchen or work on her homework or just engage in quiet, thoughtful conversation.

We worked on self-control at the same time we worked on contentment because it took self-control for her to sit still and not interrupt us during our quiet time. Instead of "punishing" her for not having the self-control to sit quietly, we noticed when she demonstrated even a little bit of it and, as a result, she started to show more of it. When I was on the phone, I asked her if she thought she could give me five minutes of uninterrupted time, and she would set the timer and wait. We stretched the time over the next few weeks and then started to talk with her about how she tended to get really loud when she got excited. We asked her if she thought she would be able to control the volume of her voice, and we came up with some nonverbal cues to encourage her. Before long, she was coming to us with ways she could demonstrate that she had self-control, like sitting at the dinner table through an entire meal without getting up or disrupting. It was like a slice of heaven when that happened.

Finally, we worked on her ability to rebound from upsets and her tenacity. We realized that our daughter is very emotionally sensitive, and her behavior was a gauge we started to use to inform us about her emotional stability. Instead of telling her to get over it, or that something was no big deal, or asking her why she was overreacting, we started to (1) show her some empathy and understanding, (2) ask her what would help her move beyond the emotion so she could come up with a solution—if it was appropriate—and (3) how we could help. She started to talk more about her feelings and articulate the things that really set her off; we were able to anticipate those triggers, and that made it possible for us to be proactive with her again. This has been life changing for all of us.

Three months after we started to work on these qualities, we were again invited to reconnect with old school friends. The car ride was delightful. Marianne brought several sticker books to work on during the long ride, and when she got bored she asked if she could listen to some music. With each song, she got louder and a little sillier. We pulled the car over, helped her through the initial meltdown brought on by her fear that we would turn around and go home, and then talked about her volume. Okay, can I say right now that my husband and I realized that we had to model the traits we were trying to teach Marianne, and this car ride demanded that we show control of our emotions and not turn into screaming lunatics, and that we could stay positive even if we had to turn around and head home, because we really wanted to attend this reunion (and if that was necessary we would be modeling resilience). As Vicki says, you can't give your kids what you don't have yourself.

Straight Talk

Although we may be able to accept the idea that we are responsible for raising future adults, it doesn't necessarily mean we know how to do that in our day-to-day interactions with our young children. The story of Marianne and her parents shows how important it is to focus on the development of character traits not just for their future selves, but because it has a positive influence in daily life with kids.

Gifts for Adulthood

Many of the parenting strategies available for tense and challenging moments with children include time-outs, counting, distracting, scolding, punishing, and giving in. But the majority of these strategies not only fracture our relationship with our kids and interfere with their drive toward independence, they do nothing to help kids develop the character traits that will support a healthy adult life and improve their current ability to deal with daily frustrations. Imagine how much happier life will be for everyone when our kids begin to tap into these essential character traits as a solution for their daily challenges. If we fail to understand the correlation between the development of character traits in young children and the presence of these positive traits in the adults they become, then we haven't fully realized the responsibility we have to our children.

By the time your child is four or five years old, you will have noticed positive traits that will make life easier for her now and when she is an adult as well as shortfalls that will make life more challenging for her throughout childhood and will create obstacles for her as an adult. These traits include self-control, forgiveness, patience, resilience, and compassion, and you will see a direct connection between a lack of character development and a lack of improvement in their behavior. **The biggest factor in diminishing conflict is the development of positive character traits in our children.**

In my work, I look for patterns of behavior. Over the years, I have found this to be universally true: if a child has a deficiency in the area of self-control and her parents do not work diligently to help develop this character trait, the child will struggle throughout her life.

CHAPTER FOUR

Your Thumbprint on the Blueprint

Now you've considered the importance of your child's relationship blueprint, the necessity that he become independent and self-reliant, ways to swiftly and accurately identify the mistaken goal of his behavior, ways you can deal with the behavior in the moment without making things worse, and the character traits you want your child to develop. With the knowledge you've gained from that reflection, it's time for the final element—designing intentional plans with your unique child(ren) and family in mind. This final element adds more power to your plan for raising capable children and competent adults. You will be designing routines and establishing boundaries that take into consideration your child's personality and idiosyncrasies, which will make each and every routine or plan seem like a perfect fit.

Your Expertise Is the Final Detail

At first, it may seem like designing routines means more work, but by the end of this chapter you'll see how the method helps you find solutions that bring about positive, peaceful, and long-lasting change. Not to mention that you will feel more connected to your child.

Without this final element parents can quickly find themselves hovering close to the edge of disaster as they maneuver through life with kids whose unique personalities and idiosyncrasies influence every routine, structure, limit, or boundary the parents try to put into place to support the family.

Building a Strong Foundation

Creating routines, structures, boundaries, and limits can make life happier, more enjoyable, and more fulfilling for parents and children without extinguishing the dynamic nature of life. On any given day, parents from every walk of life, with children ranging in age from six months to sixteen years, make on-the-spot decisions about how they will "handle" their mornings, sibling fights, homework, chores, meals, and bedtimes. These impulsive decisions often set in motion a series of unfortunate events that end with someone in tears, an escalation of a power struggle, or a misunderstanding—and, in some cases, they further fracture an already fragile parent–child relationship.

Once we understand this, the question becomes, *Why don't people more regularly institute routines, structures, boundaries, and limits?* For one, parents are afraid life will become mundane, boring, or confining. However, a real sense of freedom and ease in life comes with consistency, continuity, and predictability, all attributes that are foundational if we wish to live a balanced life. A second reason is that parents often think it's too much work. Trust me, after raising five children myself, I can attest to the fact that setting up a solid infrastructure is far less work than living by the seat of your pants and establishing new routines as you are trying to get out of the house in the morning. Clear expectations around routines make life more enjoyable for everyone and will keep parents from demanding more than their kids can reasonably deliver. It's a win for everyone. And finally, many parents simply don't know where to start. I say start right here, because if I can do this, you can too. Anyone can. Everyone can! Have faith that an investment on the front end will create more room for a positive, enjoyable connection with your children.

The Benefits

There are big benefits to living with intention versus living by the seat of your pants, making on-the-spot decisions, crossing your fingers, and hoping that the routine you adopted that morning will get you to work on time. When parents are clear about the intentional routines, structure, boundaries, and limits they put in place to support their family, children mature and grow within a healthy space that allows for order, independent thinking and decision making. This structure also provides a chance for kids to experience consequences, both positive and negative, and allows everyone in the family to become more accomplished problem solvers. Children are also afforded an opportunity to develop healthy habits and resilience when they are held accountable for their actions.

Taking the time to identify, set up, and follow through with routines, structures, limits, and boundaries is not as overwhelming as it sounds. These things work together, just like the elements of my method, to support your active and unique family. This process is both stable and fluid, and it embraces the reality that life is dynamic and that growth and change are inevitable and desirable.

Right about now you might be thinking to yourself, "That sounds great, but what are the logistics? Do you just map out a routine? How will it work for my child?" The answer is that there is no hard-and-fast template to implement. Here's why: every family has different values (i.e., nature first, then television, or sports, sports, sports, and so on). Every child has a different personality, as well as different rhythms and preferences. Every adult has different preferences too. The trick is using the facts—which are based largely on either your intuition or the patterns you have identified in yourself and your kids—to adapt the "plan" to work for your family, so that you can experience your perfect morning (not someone else's).

Structuring life with children is ultimately meant to make life easier when they are young as well as to provide them with the environment and the opportunities to develop character traits and attributes that are necessary for a healthy and happy adulthood.

The Route to Routines

Routines create a base for all intentional efforts. They can be as simple as the way you organize hats, boots, gloves, and coats during the long, snowy Vermont winters or as elaborate as my own morning routine, which accommodated seven individuals with distinct preferences and personalities. My family's goal—which, incidentally, is not the same as that of every family on our street, at our school, or in our community—was simple: to be out of the door by seven-thirty every morning. You'll notice that my expectations were reasonable in the beginning. I didn't include that everyone would have all their gear, have eaten a nutritious breakfast, and be smiling when we closed the door behind us. I started simple and grew as the family became more accustomed to the routines. Because we were a family of seven we had a rather involved situation, which included kids who would get up at four forty-five in the morning to do homework while others would be up to shower at six o'clock and another would hit the snooze button four times, slide down the banister, and just barely make it into his seat as the car was pulling away. But we made it, and that is because we established a routine and I took into consideration the unique nature of each member of the family. Did it take some time to find our sweet spot? You bet, but once we hit our stride it was smooth sailing for years.

The process of creating routines, structures, boundaries, and limits can be tailored to meet the needs of kids who struggle with time management, those who are easily frustrated or distracted, kids with special needs, and children who are part of a shared custody agreement. Routines can be designed to support a single parent or kids who move frequently as the result of a parent's career. No matter the circumstances, and no matter how unique and original your children are, every routine, once designed, can be adapted to solve a variety of problems.

Routines by Design

Revamping or creating your family's routines can be a strategic, almost exciting, challenge, a chess game of cause and effect that can bring a family closer together. The most effective routines are the result of parents taking the time to observe their kids and then "designing" a household environment that will lead to effortless routines. You're probably thinking, "Please, that's going to be hard and time consuming." But the truth is, it can be an activity that unites the family and fosters a feeling of connection and cooperation.

Before long, you'll develop a deep appreciation for the fact that your child's ability to create routines that support his individual rhythms will help him in every aspect of his life. Once again, you are investing in your long-range goal of raising high-functioning adults while taking advantage of the benefits while you live with your toddlers and teens. It's a perfect balance with a win–win outcome.

Because you are teaching your kids the skill of creating routines and systems that work for them, you are influencing their relationship blueprint by supporting and encouraging their creative genius, and at the same time you are supporting their march toward independence. What's the best part of all this? You will avoid power struggles and misunderstandings once your children are in charge of creating routines for themselves that are designed specifically for the unique individuals they are. For those of you who are still a bit nervous about handing responsibility for family routines over to your kids, take into consideration that you are also supporting those all-important character traits—ingenuity, resourcefulness, and resilience.

Here are some examples of how routines, structures, boundaries, and limits work together.

Routines organize those times of day that can throw many families into chaos and provide structure that supports the child as he develops. Routines are the umbrella that can bring order and harmony to a flurry of activity during the day.

Structures are intended to support and enforce your routines. They hold everyone accountable to the same guidelines, schedules, and expectations and can dramatically decrease confusion and grumbling by eliminating any parental involvement in executing the routine. What this means is that the structure offers a consequence when people fail to meet objectives, or when you need a guideline to stick to, so mom stays out of it (doesn't nag) and lets time teach the lesson. The trick with structures is that you have to stick to them in order to make a smooth routine. Structures include:

- Alarm clocks and timers
- Holding bins for "stuff"
- Specific times that are nonnegotiable but support decision making. (*Breakfast will be on the table at seven o'clock; if you miss it, you can make something for yourself as long as you clean up after yourself*)
- Shower schedules or bathroom schedules
- Homework calendars
- Pickups/drop-offs
- Outdoor time
- Lights out
- Technology times

Boundaries and limits help parents identify what they are and are not willing to do, which keeps confusion to a minimum and respect to a maximum. When we can identify our own boundaries and limits we can honor them and respect our kids at the same time. Imagine all the power struggles that could be avoided when the boundaries and limits are clear to everyone in the family.

- If you miss the bus once, I will drive you to school.
- If you miss the bus a second time, you can either find a ride or pay me $2.00 to drive you (this is what will happen in the real world, so why not prepare kids for the reality now).
- Everyone must have something to eat before she leaves the house, but I don't care what that something is.

Boundaries and limits also set the framework for teaching kids that as they grow and mature, the boundaries will change to match their abilities.

- Your four-year-old goes to bed at seven o'clock. She is grouchy if she stays up any later and she has difficulty getting up in the morning.

- By the time she is six years old she is able to stay up until eight o'clock with the family and still get up with the alarm clock at six thirty.
- At age nine, she is setting her own bedtime, because she has demonstrated a great deal of independence and responsibility.

This growth is possible as a result of thoughtful routines that take into account your child's abilities and the rate at which she can handle more. Think of how easy life would be if you knew ahead of time that the fights over bedtime would be solved once and for all. It's possible when you combine thoughtful routines with what you know about your one-of-a-kind child.

For me, firm routines, structures, and boundaries flushed out all the hidden trouble that could have disrupted us. Beyond that, the process taught my kids how to consider their limitations and to create healthy boundaries that they have applied to their lives as young adults.

Tiny Tweaks for Your Tot (or Teen)

It's important to remember that, in order for any routine to work for more than a week or two and benefit the family as a whole, you must incorporate your child's unique nature into the mix. As parents, we must trust our gut feelings or the intuitive sense we have about each of our kids. Even if you don't believe in gut feelings, you can observe your child and identify patterns of behavior or preferences, styles, and rhythms that will make the job of designing routines much easier. However, you mustn't be frustrated or give up if your initial design doesn't stick right away or if it doesn't work as well as you thought it might. Give each solution some time. Don't be afraid to keep going until something feels right. For example, if your child cannot manage to get homework done at night (and you know this is because you battle every night before bed), you may think, "Gee, I bet a morning rise-and-shine routine could work." If that doesn't work, you might think, "All right—Mondays, all afternoon, my child can do his entire week's math packet." Keep going until a routine tweak alleviates the stress of nightly homework battles. Then, once you find something that works, stick with it!

Many parents find it incredible that by the time their children have entered kindergarten, they can accurately predict how their kids will respond in most situations, identify whether one child is a night owl and another a morning lark, whether a child needs quiet time each day or whether she is at her best when in constant motion. I think this is the intuitive nature of parenting, and it is often either overlooked or quashed completely. And yet, in my work and certainly in my own life, I see that once this skill is cultivated—the skill of accurately predicting how your child will respond in any number of situations—your ability to parent with a sense of confidence and ease increases. Your intuitive sense of your child makes constructing intentional plans that support children incredibly simple, and it creates a frame of reference from which all decisions and responses are based.

Finding the Sweet Spot of Success

I've yet to meet a family who didn't struggle with common-area messes. Most try multiple strategies that are both creative and complicated, and almost all of these families report limited or no success in maintaining their solution for more than a few days or weeks. Here is an example of how three very different families created a routine with a structure, boundaries, and limits, and made it work for their family.

Situation: All three families identified the same daily challenge. Toys, homework, and gear were being left out in the common area, and no matter what the parents tried they couldn't get the kids to be consistent about picking up their things without a lot of nagging, reminding, coaxing, bribing, and then ultimately threatening the child with some sort of consequence. All of the parents understood that the way they were handling the common-area mess was interfering with a healthy relationship with their kids and with the kids' ability to become independent. They were willing to explore the idea of developing a well-thought-out routine, with a structure and a few boundaries and limits to support the routine's success. The following scenarios show the different ways each family addressed the challenge and used the components to come up with a routine that worked for them.

The routine: We all pick up the common area so that everyone in the family can enjoy the space without having to move someone else's stuff out of the way.

The structure: Each of the three families likes the idea of the "safe deposit box"—a secure place where items left in common areas after the designated cleanup time are stored until an appointed retrieval date. The parents all believe that this will work well in solving the challenge of kids leaving stuff around the house. The safe deposit box is the structure. Each family has different ideas for the boundaries surrounding the safe deposit box (how the system will work), and each family includes children of varying ages and temperaments. The following demonstrates how one structure can work to accommodate any family.

Family One

Boundaries: Pick up clutter by six thirty each evening. Empty once a week on Sunday morning.

Limits: None; everything left out goes into the safe deposit box for the week.

Family Two

Boundaries: Pick up clutter by seven thirty each morning. Empty at the weekly family meeting.

Limits: Mom and dad's things do not get put in the safe deposit box.

Family Three

Boundaries: Pick up Monday and Thursday at some point during the day. Empty twice a week on Tuesday and Saturday morning.

Limits: Homework and sports gear are excluded; this equipment can be left out.

Let's look at family number one and find out what their experience was like.

Marianne and Gabe shared the following:

We decided that we could live with a mess until right after dinner and that a quick sweep of the common area at that time would support the family having a stress-free, loving, and connected evening as the kids prepare for bedtime. We decided that we would empty the safe deposit out once a week after Sunday breakfast and have all the kids go through it with us and talk about the stuff that got left behind and ended up in the box. We will give the things back to each family member, donate the items family members don't want but someone that else might enjoy, or throw the item away. We all agreed as a family to try this new routine for picking up the common area for two weeks.

Here is what we learned:

- If the parents don't have to play by the same rules, the kids aren't interested in helping create any kind of routine or structure to support the family. They figured that if it was good for the kids, it was good for the adults. We couldn't really argue with them.

- Even when kids do participate in setting up the routines, there is an element of distrust that we, their parents, will actually support the routine past its honeymoon phase. They believe we will return to the yelling and nagging in short order.

- The kids are nervous about this new routine. I sense that they are so used to having no routines or structures that the idea of tuning in to them and being held accountable makes them nervous. From a long-term perspective, this is troubling. The rest of the world operates on routines, structures, boundaries, and limits.

What do you know about your children that will ensure you have set up a structure that will work for them?

This question asks you to take into account the unique nature of each of your kids and to combine it with your intuitive sense about the way they move through the world in order to support them and make adjustments to your family's routine, structure, boundaries, and limits.

Our fourteen-year-old, Sam, will take advantage of this new system the first week or two and will test our resolve by leaving his coat, boots, and most likely his backpack in the common area just to see if we are serious about this new strategy. To support his challenging nature we are prepared to put everything in the safe deposit box without comment and we will not negotiate with him, let him buy his stuff out, or send notes to the teachers that explain why he is unprepared for class. We realize that he is lacking in some of the character traits that will be necessary if he is going to make it on his own in just four short years. This is a great opportunity to help him develop those character traits and also support his "testing" nature.

Our ten-year-old, Michael, is pretty easygoing and he is by nature a pleaser. He is happiest when the family is experiencing those moments of bliss together, so if he thinks this could impact the evening in a positive way, he will be all in. Now that I think about it, I could leverage his keen sense that cooperation is at the center of most pleasant interactions and cultivate this trait in other ways. I also need to be mindful that he will pick up the slack for his brothers if they resist this new system. I'm not sure he is aware that his pattern is to pick up the slack for his brothers but then feel resentful toward them. Once he feels resentment, he starts to disconnect and it comes out in snippy, hurtful comments he makes under his breath. This triggers Sam, and before you know it, they are into a tussle. I can help Michael recognize this about himself, so he can really be at choice in those moments.

Our six-year-old son, Nate, is often ready for bed by six thirty and it's a struggle to make it through the bedtime routine without incident. You can imagine that the idea of a "clean sweep" right before bed could be his undoing. To support him I think we need to buddy up with him initially, so he understands that it will only take a few minutes, no one is angry or upset, and, in fact, the cleanup will add a more relaxing feel to the evening.

Marianne and Gabe now have a routine that includes picking up the common area on a regular basis, a structure that uses the safe deposit box to hold the items left out, boundaries that include everyone, and limits that state they can all claim their stuff on Sunday morning and not before.

The Method in Action

Here is an example of how the four elements support Marianne and Gabe as they navigate their way through this specific challenge with their fourteen-year-old son, Sam.

Step One: Describing the Situation (in as few words as possible)

This is the result of the four questions you ask yourself to determine the mistaken goal of behavior.

Gabe leaves his stuff all over the house and we are getting pretty annoyed with him, and after a few days we are downright angry. We threaten, take privileges away, pick up the junk while mumbling under our breaths, and basically feel resentful that he won't help us out. We are **angry** and threaten him, which tells us his mistaken goal is **power**.

Step Two: Evaluating the Relationship Blueprint

Identify any negative labels you use with your children, which influence their self-ideal (lazy, defiant, and disrespectful), and replace them with positive attributes/qualities you want to use so your children develop a healthy self-ideal.

Sam is quite strong-willed, passionate, and curious. Our focus on being in control has squashed any positive aspect of Sam's personality and character. We are always at odds. The parts of Sam that make it the most difficult to boss him around are the parts of him that are his greatest asset. What a relief to think he isn't easily persuaded.

What parenting strategies do you use to manipulate your children into changing their behavior and what will you replace them with?

We dictate, demand, and tighten the reins when he doesn't do what we want. I think we are treating him like a little kid instead of the man he is becoming. It is easy to say, "He is acting like a baby, so why shouldn't we treat him like one," but the truth of the matter is, we started this cycle, not him. His defiance is telling us something and it is time we listen. We are going to start by realizing he is a capable young man and invite him into the conversation and ask him to help us with family policy. Once we have some insight from him, we will be able to move forward.

What qualities of a healthy relationship do you want to focus on that, over time, will influence or change this scenario in a positive way and support qualities found in a healthy relationship?

We sat down and thought about all the qualities we consider crucial in a healthy relationship and realized that we hadn't done a real good job modeling any of them for our kids. We talked about them, sure, but model them for the boys? Not so much. Instead of creating a list that had no real meaning for us, we decided to spend a week noticing the ways we treated each other, our friends, and our coworkers and create our list from that experience. From there, we identified three words that had meaning for us and we wrote down exactly how we would support these words through our actions. We have no doubt that as soon as we start modeling these words instead of paying lip service to them, all our relationships are going to improve.

Compassion: Modeling compassion with our kids means accepting where they are in the learning process. We can't compare them to one another or to other people. We have to accept who they are and where they are in their journey of life, and have compassion for the areas in their lives that are difficult for them. I want my kids to have compassion for themselves, so they don't end up being dissatisfied with the lives they built and I want them to extend that same courtesy to others who may be struggling.

Quiet confidence: I think this is a quality that is often overlooked, but when you recognize it in other people, you know right away that they have something special. It's not that braggart kind of confidence, it's the quiet confidence that comes from knowing that you know yourself and you can handle life's ups and downs. I want the kids to have confidence in their ability to make decisions, even if those decisions lead to momentary disasters. I want them to have confidence in their ability to bounce back from upsets and disappointments. In order for that to happen we have to have confidence in our parenting and show confidence in them now. It's as simple as supporting the clothes they choose to wear, the music they listen to, the way they make their sandwiches, how they solve their problems. I guess what I am saying is, we have to have faith in them so they can have confidence in themselves.

Mutual respect: We had to spend some time thinking about the "mutual" part of this quality. We know that mutual respect is crucial in healthy relationships, but we weren't sure if we were showing respect for ourselves when we stooped to nagging and coaxing and harassing a fourteen-year-old kid. Obviously, we weren't. In order to model mutual respect we have to remain firm and kind, follow through with what we say, stay connected throughout the week, and model respect for his choice to test the system.

Step Three: Fostering Independence

Have you been supporting his independence in this area?

Because we so often ended up fighting with him and then giving in around his messes, we interfered with his learning to take care of his own stuff without reminders. By following through, we are fostering his independence and allowing him to take full responsibility for organizing his life.

How will you foster your child's independence in a way that will influence this situation and ensure he is independent and self-sufficient when he is an adult?

Timeline for training: Going through the exercise was a wake-up call. We were interfering so often in areas we had no business even commenting on that we had to go back and start with self skills. Can you imagine that we were still reminding our son to take a shower? Embarrassing. We have a plan for how to make sure that our son has ample time to master all four areas—self, home, social, and life skills before he leaves in four short years. We sat down with him and talked honestly about what we would step away from, which skills he still needed a bit of support in, and which skills we hadn't even touched on. We have a new focus for our relationship now, and that's exciting to all of us.

Privileges and responsibilities: Because of Sam's personality, this is going to be the most effective and respectful way to organize our lives together. We can't change the rules just because we are upset with Sam, and he can't blame us when a privilege is revoked because he didn't assume the responsibility that goes along with it. In the case of the safe deposit box, he will have to decide if testing and losing his gear is more important than accepting this new structure and putting his energy into making it work for him. This is going to be a learning experience for Sam.

Step Four: Living with a Teen

What can you do in the moment that would move the action forward without making things worse?

- Say what we mean, mean what we say, and do it.
- Remain firm and kind.
- Walk away from his invitations to get into a debate about the safe deposit box.

Step Five: Raising an Adult

What character traits or life lessons can you teach in this situation that will benefit your child from age eighteen to eighty?

I just want to go on record as saying that this exercise highlights so many character traits and life lessons we want to teach our kids that we would have overlooked otherwise. Now, instead of resorting to our usual nagging, reminding, and threatening tactics, we think about what trait we want to help our kids develop, and our mood changes immediately. We are being proactive instead of reactive, and we are prioritizing accordingly.

Thinking ahead: We know in our own lives that the ability to think beyond the moment helps us make informed decisions and often redirects our actions and attitudes. We had been thinking ahead for them, which is why there was so much pushback. We identified a number of situations, beginning first thing in the morning, where we could support this particular trait in our son (and other kids). We started with the morning—"What happens if you sleep through your alarm clock?" Instead of telling him what would happen, we started to ask all the kids, "So what will happen if..." They were instantly engaged and started to predict how things would go for them, and then they started to modify their choices, and then the most remarkable thing happened—they started to take responsibility for those choices.

Prioritizing: There is only so much time in any given day, and a person only has so much energy, so it's important to learn how to prioritize. If you don't, it's easy to get overwhelmed with life and to put the things most important to you at the bottom of your daily to-do list. Gabe and I experienced this in our marriage. When our marriage stopped being our number-one priority, it started to crumble.

The kids are learning that when they leave certain items out repeatedly, that it's time to discard them. Those things no longer have the same meaning for them that they once did. It's amazing how much the kids are learning and how they are applying this skill to other areas of their lives.

For instance, the other night one of the kids was getting really upset with his brother and lashing out, calling him names and being really hurtful. I pulled him aside, sat down with him till he was calm, and then said, "You have to decide what's more important to you—hurting your brother right now in this moment or taking the time to calm down and talking to him because you love him and he loves you. Only you can decide." There was this moment of complete clarity in his eyes. He snuffled a few more times, sat by himself for a few more minutes, and then came out of his room and said, "I don't like it when you tease me. Can you just show me how to do the card trick?" Boom. He hit the target. His brother was immediately touched by the honesty and they went on to have a wonderful time together. Now, I don't expect this will happen all the time, but it shows us how powerful identifying these character traits can be in helping us foster a healthy home environment.

Step Six: Creating an Intentional Plan

Describe the routine, structure, or plan you want to implement.

The safe deposit box—see above.

Step Seven: Trusting Your Intuition

What do you know about your child that ensures you have set up a structure that will work for him?

This is a kid who constantly tests the boundaries, and in the past we have been really angry with him for not just going along with what we said. We will be prepared for him to test this system and won't get drawn into the battle. What we also know about him, and what we haven't appreciated, is that once he is convinced that a system or routine, or consequence for that matter, isn't going to change, he accepts it, adapts quickly, and, for the most part, goes along with it nicely.

Putting These Steps to Work for You

Following these steps and constructing tailored approaches for each child could take a bit of time initially, but with practice and a commitment to your kids, to your family, and to this method, you will find that over just a few weeks it will become easier to integrate the four elements. Before long, you will notice that you are using the same descriptions for your kids, which makes the method even more effective. You are using accurate information, not just guessing about your motives and your goals, and you become more confident in considering the unique nature of each of your kids when you construct a plan.

You will also find that, although some of the relationship qualities you want to develop in the kids are different, they often overlap. Before long, you and your partner will be focusing on one or two important qualities in all of the kids until you see progress and improvement. You will also notice this same pattern when it comes to the character traits you are trying to foster in the kids.

What will change is the way you deal with each of your children in the moment, but that is far easier than re-creating ineffective, haphazard plans with no other considerations in mind. In my own life with kids, I decided to commit thirty days to working with this method in written form. I had large pieces of paper on the wall in my bedroom marked with step one, step two, and so on, so that I could fill it out and see where I was getting stuck. This immediately identified for me the areas that required more effort and the areas that were working. For me, the intuitive part was the easiest, so I worked from there. If I knew I had a morning lark who wanted to do homework at five o'clock in the morning and I was working on creating a routine for the entire family, I plugged that piece in first and built around what I knew about each of the kids. Other parts of the method took more time for me to master.

Another benefit of teaching myself this method and taking the time to practice it was that I had a new appreciation for what my kids were going through each day in their own lives. Kids are learning so many things at the same time, and sometimes parents pile on tasks, skills, and expectations that finally send them over the edge. Showing myself compassion and allowing myself to practice, to fail, to try again, and to finally feel the excitement of successfully mastering a new skill flowed over into my parenting, and suddenly I was a friendlier, more patient, and more encouraging parent. Who knew that by exercising my own mental muscle I would begin to parent more regularly from my best self?

The elements of the method are listed below, to help you see just how easy it is to fill in the blanks. Yet you can also see just how specific this method is and why it can work for any family with any number of children ranging in age from infancy to nearly out the door, all of whom have different preferences, personalities, and ways of moving through the world.

Practice Steps One Through Seven

Take this opportunity to use a challenge from your own life and follow along.

Step One: Describing the Situation (in as few words as possible)

This is the result of the four questions you ask yourself to determine the mistaken goal of behavior.

Step Two: Evaluating the Relationship Blueprint

Identify any negative labels you use with your children, which influence their self-ideal, and replace them with positive attributes/qualities you want to use so your children develop a healthy self-ideal.

Be as honest as you can when you identify the negative labels you use with your children. You may want to take a day or two and write down the negative words you use to describe your children. Include both the ones you say out loud and the ones in your head.

When we focus on the moments of conflict or what we would like to change about our children, we tend to identify them with labels that do little to help foster courage and a desire to connect. Our children are not their pesky behaviors. Our children are doing the best they can with the information they have. Our job as parents is to shift our perspective, identify our children's strengths, and build on those strengths.

Think about the words you would like your child to use to describe himself as a young adult. Begin to incorporate these words into daily life with your children, pointing out when they are demonstrating these attributes or traits so that they begin to identify with them. In this way, you are fostering a healthy self-ideal in your children. As a result, they will look for other people who also demonstrate these same positive attributes.

What parenting strategies do you use to manipulate your children into changing their behavior and what will you replace them with?

Remember that your children will use the same kinds of strategies when they interact with those outside their family. Consider the strategies you use to manipulate your children into doing what you want. You might bark orders, let them know you are disappointed in them, bribe them, withhold affection, or threaten them with a loss of a favorite toy or a privilege. There are any number of positive strategies a parent can use to help teach kids about healthy interactions between people even when they disagree, have different perspective or styles, or need to communicate about a difficult topic. These positive strategies teach our kids about healthy relationship with people who experience the world in different ways and ensure that they will attract other people who also have a strong sense of how to interact with others respectfully and cooperatively.

What qualities of a healthy relationship do you want to focus on that, over time, will influence or change this scenario in a positive way and support qualities found in a healthy relationship?

Identify qualities that have meanings you may not be accurately communicating and decide how you will better model the values that you say are so important.

The goal is to identify two or three qualities that you think are important in a healthy relationship and how you will begin to model them and introduce them.

Step Three: Fostering Independence

Have you been fostering independence in your child?

The goal is to consider whether you have been creating a home environment that fosters independence in your child. Sniff out all the ways that you might be interfering with your child's ability to become more self-sufficient.

How do you want to foster her independence in this situation and ensure that she continues to grow more independent over time? This is often subtle and can be hard to identify.

The goal is to identify specific ways that you can foster independence in daily life with your child. You can use the strategies suggested in chapter 2, and you can always add your own unique strategies.

Step Four: Living with a Toddler/School-Aged Child/Teen

What can you do in the moment that will move the action forward without making things worse?

The goal is to move the action forward without creating more difficulties. You can think about a long-term strategy when you are calm. This is not a teachable moment if your emotions have already been activated.

Step Five: Raising an Adult

What character traits or life lessons can you teach in this situation that will benefit your child from age eighteen to eighty?

The goal is to identify character traits that will both serve your child in adulthood and help him deal with the daily challenges of life. Nurturing healthy character traits in our children is like a marathon. Pacing ourselves, keeping the right mind-set, and keeping our eye on the prize will make this element of my method both immediately satisfying and beneficial in the long term.

Step Six: Creating an Intentional Plan

Describe the routine, structure, or plan you want to implement.

The goal is to identify routines, structures, boundaries and limitations that will add a quality of organization and stability to your life with kids. It's also a great way to model for the kids the value of creating routines or other intentional plans that they can use in their own life as adults.

Step Seven: Trusting Your Intuition

What do you know about your child that ensures you have set up a structure that will work for him?

The goal is to identify unique qualities in your children that will ensure that the plan you create will support them. For instance if your child is a morning lark you might want to consider allowing him to do his homework in the morning instead of forcing him to do it in the evening when he is tired and distracted.

Here We Go: Theory to Practice

Parenting isn't a science, but if we know what to look for and we can gather and assimilate information, we are in a position to get the most out of every day, creating a deep sense that we are enjoying our young children and still preparing them for life beyond our threshold.

In part 2 you will be introduced to eighteen families with children ranging in age from two to sixteen. They will share their experiences tackling one of eight common parenting challenges using the method I have introduced in part 1. I encourage you to read each of the stories and allow yourself to think about your life as a family and how you can apply this method to facilitate change and invest in the relationship you are creating with your children.

PART TWO

Stories from the Heart

Over the past twenty-five-years I have worked with countless parents, offering support as they navigate the sometimes difficult, often mysterious, always thrilling work of creating a healthy environment for raising capable, cooperative, responsible, and respectful children (or, in other words, for growing a grown-up). When I first studied Adlerian psychology as a new mother, I developed a method for my personal use that kept me out of the meandering stories from friends about what wasn't working, how frustrated they were, and how miserable life with the kids had become. Not every story sounded like that, but there were enough of them that I knew I needed a plan to get through all the drama. As I asserted in *Duct Tape Parenting*, I was not willing to fight with my children for eighteen years.

Adlerian psychology trains us to identify a problem quickly, so we as parents and educators can put our time and energy into finding solutions that will facilitate long-term change. I soon realized that my interpretation of the work of Alfred Adler and Rudolf Dreikurs established a framework that supported the method I was using to navigate my way through my own parenting journey. As a parent educator, I began to teach parents each step of the method and then work with them until they felt confident using it without me. It wasn't long before these parents didn't need me at all, and in my line of work that signals a resounding success. My core belief is that parents are the true experts in their children's lives and my goal as a teacher and coach is to help them uncover their expertise and put it to use.

I believe that storytelling, particularly as it applies to parenting, is one of the most powerful tools we have for understanding new concepts, ideas, and strategies. I encourage the families I work with to keep a journal to track progress and keep their perspective fresh. Stories are also beneficial for parents who are eager to leverage the experience of others and take advantage of new ways of interacting with their children.

When I asked these families if they would be willing to share their journals and personal experiences describing the ups and downs of using the method as well as their results, the benefits, and the aha moments they experienced, they happily agreed. To protect the families and their identities, we have changed their names and identifying features, however, the ages of the children, their language, and, most importantly, their awareness, observations, and insights have been reprinted directly from their experience. My hope is that you will see how this method was used by real parents raising real kids in the twenty-first century and how, with a bit of practice, they learned to adapt some of the elements to better support their particular family dynamic. I hope these stories challenge your thinking and offer you new ways of looking at common parenting challenges. More than anything, though, I hope they inspire you to dream big and to step into that uncomfortable place we call change and try something new.

Part 2 is a collection of stories from parents with children ranging in age from two to sixteen, and it covers the nine most common parenting challenges. The first part of each story is the initial account or point of contact from the parents. From there, it's a matter of each set of parents working each element of the method until they have a clear understanding of the problem and a solution tailor-made for their family, based solely on the information they provide. Although initially my role was to ask parents to challenge some of their ideas or to go deeper into a question, after only two or three working sessions, most parents were able to do the work on their own. You will notice in step one that words and feelings are highlighted in each story to help you connect the feeling with the problem, which is an essential component of these stories.

After a few stories, you may see patterns emerging.

1. The parents are required to look at themselves and evaluate their own behavior.

2. Many of the changes parents are looking for within the family start with the changes they are willing to make in their own parenting approach.

3. It is clear that the changes they are looking to make in their families will happen slowly, over time. These parents, like most of the parents I work with, are anxious and excited for change, and that is understandable. However, it's important to remember that you are working on your child's timeline, not yours. So be patient with yourself and with your kids when you're implementing this method.

4. There are strategies parents can use in the moment of conflict or strife that will move the action forward without making things worse. Remember that lasting change requires time and commitment, and that the moments of intense frustration are *not* teachable moments. They are moments for you to gather information about the progress you are making with your children, to understand where to focus your efforts, and to celebrate the improvement you see.

Enjoy these stories and use the page in the book or the downloadable document available at vickihoefle.com to jot down any ideas or thoughts that come to you while you are reading the bedtime bedlam story or any other story in part 2. There is nothing wrong with leveraging another parent's insights and ideas. After all, most of us have the same goal: to enjoy our children while they are young and to raise adults we would be proud to call our friends.

CHAPTER FIVE

Bedtime Bedlam

A battle-free bedtime is every parent's dream; but when we lose track of the big picture, cave to our children's tears and tantrums, and usher kids up the stairs relying on a hope and a prayer for a happier ending to the day, we doom ourselves and our kids to another night of Bedtime Bedlam.

Toddler

Caroline and her three-year-old daughter, Kate, are struggling with disastrous bedtime routines and are perpetuating a cycle Caroline can't seem to break. Caroline shared the following:

I am exhausted after a long day, and by bedtime I am ready to tuck Kate in, sing her a song, kiss her goodnight, and head downstairs for some time to myself, but Kate has always had trouble sleeping. In fact, for the first year of her life I could only get her to sleep if I was holding her and then for the next two years I laid on her floor almost every night until she fell asleep. Now, at three, I feel like she is old enough to go to bed on her own after a short bedtime ritual, but it does not matter what I think, our routine goes on forever. I will get Kate tucked in and then she wants to use the bathroom or she cries for me to kiss her one more time or she begs for a sip of water, and this litany of requests goes on for another fifteen minutes. When I finally do get out of the room, it's not unusual for her to come out of her room a dozen times during the night. I am fed up and

I am taking my frustration out on her. I have tried bribing, negotiating, giving in, and doling out consequences, but nothing works to change the dynamic in any meaningful or lasting way.

Step One: Describing the Situation (in as few words as possible)

This is the result of the four questions you ask yourself to determine the mistaken goal of behavior.

My three-year-old, Kate, extends the bedtime routine (a word I use loosely at this point) and I am **frustrated and tired**, so I either give in to her demands, bargain with her, or impose some consequence. The next night we repeat the same thing. This tells me that the mistaken goal of her behavior is **attention**. Boy, am I giving it to her.

Step Two: Developing a Relationship Blueprint

Identify any negative labels you use with your children that influence their self-ideal.

As Kate's mother I tend to focus on her misbehavior and I label her as demanding, stubborn, and exhausting.

Replace the negative labels with positive attributes/qualities you want to use so your children develop a healthy self-ideal.

My child knows her own mind and if I focus on this being a healthy attribute in a healthy relationship, I can foster it without getting annoyed and frustrated with her. I can teach her how to express this in a respectful way. The same goes with her tenacity when it means she is holding her own ground without bulldozing through someone else. I will focus more on creating a cooperative home environment with healthy communication skills to assist all of us in our daily interactions. I'll stop saying that she is exhausting. I am exhausted because I haven't considered a thoughtful parenting plan for myself and I am blaming my three-year-old for that.

What parenting strategies do you use to manipulate your children into changing their behavior and what will you replace them with?

We currently use bribing, negotiating, giving in, and punishing. If I imagine Kate as an adult who believes she can manipulate people into doing what she wants, I could easily imagine her bullying them until they give in to her demands since she sees me model this. I also imagine she could punish those close to her with emotional distance or by hurting them with her words. I have to start employing choices in her daily life so she learns about give-and-take, and I need to follow through on what I say without getting angry with her because she tests my resolve. I also have to start trying some of the things she suggests, even though I know they won't work very well. If I want her to be flexible with other people and try their suggestions, I have to be willing to do that with her now.

What qualities of a healthy relationship do you want to focus on that, over time, will influence or change this scenario in a positive way and support qualities found in a healthy relationship?

Cooperation: I was in control of the bedtime routine. I was making all the decisions about how it would be and modeling controlling behavior, even though I would use the word cooperate during our interactions. When I switched my thinking, it was suddenly obvious how to model a more cooperative attitude around our bedtime routine. It didn't mean that I was letting Kate make all the decisions, it meant that I would include her in more of the discussions about bedtime and allow her to be part of the decision-making process. We would now work together to design a bedtime routine that supported both of our needs.

Step Three: Fostering Independence

Have you been supporting her independence in this area?

I never considered that I was interfering with her ability to become independent in this area by catering to her demands.

How will you foster your child's independence in a way that will influence this situation and ensure she is independent and self-sufficient when she is an adult?

I looked for opportunities throughout the day to foster her budding independence. I now encourage her to try things on her own before I come and help her—which is easy because she struggles at most everything she tries. I started saying things like, "Kate, you put on your own bike helmet. That is a tricky thing to do and you did it!" Or when she has a semi-meltdown because she can't get her shoe on and she starts screaming, "I caaaaaaan't get my shoe all the way ooooooon!" I use some of Vicki's favorite lines: "What can you do with that shoe, Kate? Show me what part of your foot you can get in." Kate refocuses her energy and, sure enough, she gets half of her foot in, feels successful, and is willing to keep going. Now, this might seem simple, but when you consider that this happens more than a dozen times a day, it adds up. As Kate's confidence in her own abilities grows, I see this new confidence influencing the bedtime routine.

I invited Kate to help me more, which is something I was avoiding because she couldn't complete tasks the way I wanted her to or she was too slow or messy. I quickly learned that Kate likes to be included and that she is excited to try new things. Teaching her new skills is another way for us to connect and is an opportunity for me to teach her the art of practice and patience.

I also taught Kate how to brush her teeth, get her water, and turn her light on and off, so that when we revamped the bedtime routine she would know how to do all of these things without me and they wouldn't be included in the routine at all. Just thinking about empowering Kate to master these simple tasks set my heart to singing. It is making both of our lives easier.

When Vicki reminds us that the situation we are trying to solve is just a symptom of an underlying problem, I now understand what she means.

Step Four: Living with a Toddler

What can you do in the moment that will move the action forward without making things worse?

- Be clear about what I will do and what I won't do and then follow through.
- Stop talking. This is my biggest trip-up. I know that once I start talking I make the situation worse, so staying quiet and calm is imperative in these moments.
- Take Kate back to bed as many times as I need to without getting angry until she understands that I am serious and I follow through on what I say. Once again, this is an integral part of a healthy relationship, saying what you mean and then doing it.

Step Five: Raising an Adult

What character traits or life lessons can you teach in this situation that will benefit your child from age eighteen to eighty?

Security: I want Kate to feel secure in her life as an adult, and a big part of cultivating that sense of security is her ability to let go of the day and settle into bed without fighting it or wanting loads of attention to avoid it. Vicki had me do an exercise that really drove this home for me. She asked me to fast-forward five years and describe how, at eight years old, Kate might feel about being dropped off at soccer camp. At thirteen, how she would cope if friends at school excluded her? At eighteen, how would she feel when it was time for her to go to college? Would she be secure enough to travel cross-country to attend the college of her dreams, or would she choose to stay close to home and her local friends? It hit me that helping Kate grow in confidence and independence around bedtime will influence her sense of security in every aspect of her life.

Step Six: Creating an Intentional Plan

Describe the routine, structure or plan you want to implement.

I wanted to cut the routine by at least twenty minutes, so I analyzed our current routine and gathered information to create a new, more efficient, and more enjoyable routine for the both of us. Kate and I decided that I would help her get her pajamas on after she brushed her teeth and she was in her room. I decided I was willing to sing two songs or read one book, but not both. She would choose. I would give her a kiss, say goodnight, and leave the room. She wanted to turn off the light when I left. She was happy to be able to incorporate the new skills she had mastered into the routine. If she came out of the room for any reason, I would walk her back to her room without saying anything.

Once we decided on the new routine, we made an agreement to practice for seven days. Even now, four months into this, I can see that this solid structure allows me a chance to assess Kate's growth and to make adjustments to the routine that are in line with her growth and maturity. No more guessing or changing the routine completely, which only confuses the situation. I am now centered and calm when bedtime rolls around, which has a huge impact on the entire evening.

Step Seven: Trusting Your Intuition

What do you know about your child that will ensure you have set up a structure that will work for her?

By the time Kate is five years old, she is going to want more autonomy around this routine. She may want to read in bed or listen to music or keep the light on longer than I would like her to. I will honor her requests to let go of the day in a way that continues to make her feel secure in her life, supports her independence, and strengthens our relationship.

> **Note from Vicki:** After a few months, bedtime has improved dramatically and, not surprisingly, so have many other areas of Kate and Caroline's life. It's not perfect, but Caroline isn't looking for perfection any longer. With a focus on deepening her relationship with Kate, fostering independence, building character traits, and creating routines that are specific to Kate's personality and temperament, Caroline doesn't bother herself with things like perfection.

Teens

Margaret's fifteen-year-old daughter, Hannah, is really pushing the limits lately. She has a boyfriend, and Margaret recently discovered that Hannah has been staying up very late talking on the phone with him. Margaret says:

Hannah is not getting enough sleep, and is totally distracted and starry-eyed over this new boyfriend. She is on another planet half the time. She is lying to us about going to bed, saying goodnight, turning out the lights and music, and leading us to believe she is getting a good night's sleep. I have come to find out that she is talking on the phone until after midnight on a regular basis. The lying is unacceptable and it is totally ridiculous for a fifteen-year-old to think she has the right to stay up until midnight on a school night. If she was up and pleasant and perky in the morning, I would not mind, but she's dragging around like a wet noodle and snaps when we speak to her. We decided to take her phone away to let her know that we mean business. I have a feeling that's not going to solve the lying problem but I had to do something to get this under control before it gets any worse.

Step One: Describing the Situation (in as few words as possible)

This is the result of the four questions you ask yourself to determine the mistaken goal of behavior.

My fifteen-year-old daughter has been staying on the phone with her new boyfriend until after midnight on school nights and lies about it when we confront her. The last time I caught her in a lie I blew up, took her phone away, and considered other consequences as well. **I am angry** with her and feeling as though my authority in my home is being threatened. The only solutions I can come up with are considered punishments. I still don't understand why punishment isn't a viable option. She is lying and acting irresponsibly. I can't let her get away with this behavior. I want to show her that I am still the boss. This tells me the mistaken goal of her behavior is **power**.

Step Two: Developing a Relationship Blueprint

Identify any negative labels you use with your children that influence their self-ideal.

I am really angry with my daughter and feel she is deceitful, untrustworthy, selfish, immature, and unreasonable.

Replace the negative labels with positive attributes/qualities you want to use so your children develop a healthy self-ideal.

I will drop every single negative label and begin to identify the real essence of my child. I am so off base with those labels and, as hard as this assignment was to do, it brought to light just why things have deteriorated the way they have. She is insightful and knows her own mind. She is trusting and determined. My job is to encourage those attributes I already see in her and then help her develop mutual respect and better communication skills. If I start noticing and acknowledging when she demonstrates those two attributes, it will help her identify with them more.

What parenting strategies do you use to manipulate your children into changing their behavior and what will you replace them with?

I threaten her, punish her by taking away things that are important to her, and try to buy her good behavior by promising her things she wants, if she will do what I want her to do. I can certainly understand how Hannah could come to the conclusion that these are acceptable ways of getting what you want from the people you are in relationship with and I also know that they will not work. These methods will make it difficult for Hannah to have healthy adult relationships. Healthy relationships include collaboration and mutual respect, and if I am clear about how I want to model those with Hannah in our daily interactions, it will give her a basis for doing the same with others. I am also going to have to admit that she is getting older and will want a bigger say in how she constructs her life.

What qualities of a healthy relationship do you want to focus on that, over time, will influence or change this scenario in a positive way and support qualities found in a healthy relationship?

Mutual respect: I've learned a few things over the last few days. First, I don't demonstrate self-respect so Hannah doesn't have a role model and, second, I treat her disrespectfully and then justify my behavior. I demand respect from her and the truth is, she gives me back what I give her. I know it's going to be hard to change overnight, but I am determined to work with my daughter so that we can both develop respect for ourselves and for each other, and that starts with an honest conversation and an effort to work together to solve this challenge.

Step Three: Fostering Independence

Have you been supporting her independence in this area?

It's obvious I was treating Hannah like a baby instead of the incredibly mature, thoughtful, and intelligent person she is.

How will you foster your child's independence in a way that will influence this situation and ensure she is independent and self-sufficient when she is an adult?

Together, we made a list of all the areas of her life that she could take complete responsibility for. I agreed to take a step back and allow her the time to practice, make mistakes, and try again until she mastered all of them. This wasn't as hard as I thought it would be, because we had a plan. I would practice acknowledging her feelings, asking questions, keeping my advice to myself, and just sitting with her when that is all she wanted. My new role was to support her, not dictate play.

Once I could be trusted as an ally we tackled the areas of her life she knew little about, but that she would be expected to manage when she left home, like budgets and culinary skills. Instead of dreading the process, we are using our time together as a way to define our new and improved relationship.

Step Four: Living with a Teen

What can you do in the moment that will move the action forward without making things worse?

- Remain firm and kind.
- Follow through on the agreement and remove the phone if she is using it after ten o'clock at night.
- If I am sure she is lying, let her know and state calmly, "We will discuss this later when I have had time to think about your decision and we can discuss this without an emotional reaction." That statement alone helps Hannah take responsibility for the lying and she now feels safe enough and respected enough to tell me what's really going on. I feel a sense of calm confidence as soon as I say that I am going to think about the situation instead of just exploding and acting like a thoughtless parent.

Step Five: Raising an Adult

What character traits or life lessons can you teach in this situation that will benefit your child from age eighteen to eighty?

Courage: If Hannah is going to make choices that will break agreements and trust, then I want her to have the courage to own up to the choices she makes and...

Personal responsibility: ...take responsibility for those choices without lying, blaming, or making excuses.

Ability to stand up for herself: If I had listened to her and offered her a chance to develop her voice, by age fifteen she would know how to stand up for herself in a respectful way and wouldn't feel compelled to lie. She would have developed the courage she needs in these situations.

I want my daughter to know that I understand her, and that she can trust me and come to me with anything, but I can't just expect her to feel that way if I don't prove it with my actions. It is my turn to give her more respect, privacy, and responsibility, and to trust her to solve her own problems by staying out of her challenges. Vicki offers parents of toddlers the wisdom to stand one step behind and a half a step back. This applies to me, even though Hannah is a teen. It is never too late to show faith in your child.

Step Six : Creating an Intentional Plan

Describe the routine, structure, or plan you want to implement.

Bedtime routine: When Vicki asked me to create a bedtime routine, it was like getting a wake-up call. "Do you really mean a bedtime routine for my fifteen-year-old daughter?" I thought, "Are you nuts?" But I was still treating Hannah like she either needed one or that she should still be using the one I created for her when she was five years old.

What seemed reasonable to me was simple:

- Hannah will choose a bedtime that will allow her to get adequate sleep to function at her best the next day. I have no idea how much sleep she needs right now. I haven't been paying any attention to how she really functions, so having me set a bedtime is ridiculous. In three years she is going to be at college and will have to figure it out on her own. I feel better about her practicing now, while she is still living at home with me. She will stay on top of her responsibilities, which includes school, family contributions, and sports commitments. If she does this, we will never mention bedtime again.
- If she is not able to follow through, I will ask her to identify where things are breaking down and if there is anything I can do to support her. At fifteen years old she has the solution. It is my job to help her discover it.

Phone plan: Had I understood this information earlier, I would have created a plan for phone use before I gave her one. I missed the boat and now Hannah and I have developed some bad habits. Here is our new starting point:]

- Hannah will pay $30.00 a month toward her phone bill. This is important, because I am not going to be a parent paying her twenty-eight-year-old daughter's bills. I never would have made this connection if I hadn't done this exercise. Now I know I can hold firm on this plan, because I know it is going to benefit Hannah as an adult. Before this exercise, this was one of my punishment ideas; demand she pay me or take the phone away because she isn't paying me.

- Talk to Hannah about a part-time job. Eventually, she will start taking over more of her financial responsibilities. Her occasional babysitting jobs will pay for her phone, but when she starts driving she will be asked to pay for gas, at the very least. By stepping back and looking at her as the mature young woman she is growing into, I can see all of the possible ways she can empower herself.

- I have been so wishy-washy about the phone policy. We agreed that a good starting point is that she brings the phone to the kitchen by ten o'clock at night. This way we will build trust back, and if she is willing to do this, then within a few months, I will let her take complete responsibility for managing it.

Step Seven: Trusting Your Intuition

What do you know about your child that will ensure you have set up a structure that will work for her?

Hannah has a lot of confidence in her ability to make her own decisions. She pushes back hard when someone tries to control her, which is exactly what was happening around the phone issue. I need to remember that the more involved she is in the decision-making process, the more cooperative she will be with the decisions and agreements.

Here is what I know: my daughter wants me to trust her. I can show her in our everyday interactions that I have complete faith in her. When we establish these plans and implement privileges and responsibilities, it takes the pressure off and I stop micromanaging, punishing, and lecturing, which gets in the way of the relationship I want to have with her. I'm here to help her navigate her life while she is still in the house and let her practice. I will not expect that she'll never make a mistake or stay up late talking to a boy. This opens the door for my girl to be able to come and talk to me about the boy she is in love with—today anyway—instead of drawing a line in the sand where she ends up believing that I am her enemy. We are finding a great balance in our mother–daughter relationship.

CHAPTER SIX

Don't Throw Your Peas

Picky palates and lousy table manners can turn any family meal into a fight-fest instead of a bonding experience. Knowing what a crucial role family meals play in creating a healthy family environment, these two families were ready to challenge some of their assumptions and make a few necessary adjustments.

Toddlers

Claire's three-year-old son, Tyler, is a very picky eater and is beginning to demonstrate poor table manners. She says:

He refuses to eat most everything I cook and usually has a meltdown about it. He'll cry his way through dinner, whining about not liking the food, pushing his plate around, and getting up and down from the table. We've let Tyler know that this is not acceptable behavior at the dinner table and had to give him a time-out in the middle of dinner, but he just has a full-on temper tantrum until I end up pouring him a bowl of cereal. I don't know what else to do. I want him to have good table manners and I want him to eat a healthy dinner. What kind of mom would I be if I let him go to bed hungry? I really end up with no choice but to give in, so he will eat and stay seated at the table. I imagine how lovely a family dinner could be, and this is not it.

Step One: Describing the Situation (in as few words as possible)

This is the result of the four questions you ask yourself to determine the mistaken goal of behavior.

My three-year-old son, Tyler, refuses to eat what I cook for him. He takes over the meal with tears and tantrums and then finally leaves the table. I coax, bribe, and cater to his requests because I don't want him to go hungry. I am **frustrated and exhausted** from the shenanigans, and this tells me his mistaken goal of behavior is **attention**.

Step Two: Developing a Relationship Blueprint

Identify any negative labels you use with your children that influence their self-ideal.

I do think of my child as whiny, stubborn, demanding, challenging, and rigid. I expect him to show up and act this way every day. I see that I get what I expect.

Replace the negative labels with positive attributes/qualities you want to use so your children develop a healthy self-ideal.

He knows his own mind and is flexible, cooperative, and easy-going. Those are new ways of describing my child and I can see how finding opportunities to point out the times when he is actually behaving in those ways will help him see himself in this new way. He may continue to be a stubborn kid, but I can point out the positive ways his tenacity serves him and others. I just didn't know I could turn the meaning into something positive.

What parenting strategies do you use to manipulate your children into changing their behavior and what will you replace them with?

Time-outs, lectures, and showing him my disapproval. I can imagine that Tyler could easily come to believe that it is acceptable to manipulate people into doing what he wants by showing his disapproval of them or their actions, and even acting in a superior way and lecturing other people when they don't behave the way he thinks they should. By incorporating healthier and more respectful ways of parenting, I can model for him how to solve conflicts and live more coopera- tively with others. This will serve him now and in the future. Thankfully, Vicki provides a suite of respectful and effective solutions for me to draw from. My reluctance in the past has been that they are hard for me to implement and they take time, but what else is more important than helping my child build a founda- tion for healthy future relationships?

What qualities of a healthy relationship do you want to focus on that, over time, will influence or change this scenario in a positive way and support qualities found in a healthy relationship?

Trust: I had to think about this one as it applies to a three-year-old. I realize I have to model behavior that teaches Tyler to trust me and that means I have to say what I mean, mean what I say, and then do it. I think if Tyler knew that I was serious about how I handled the meal disruptions his behavior would improve. Because he can't trust how I will handle the next meal, his behavior is all over the place. I want Tyler to trust that he can make good decisions in difficult situa- tions, trust his assessment of people and situations, and trust that he can handle challenging life events. If I can remember that following through with what I say teaches Tyler about trust, this will give me the strength to get through those moments when I worry that he will be hungry.

Step Three: Fostering Independence

Have you been supporting his independence in this area?

I didn't even consider the idea that, as a parent, I was supposed to be support- ing his independence. I just thought it was my job as his mother to do every- thing for him until he was older. That question sure is a wake-up call for me to change the way I think and how I spend my time with him.

How will you foster your child's independence in a way that will influence this situation and ensure he is independent and self-sufficient when he is an adult?

- Allow Tyler to help create the dinner menu.
- Teach him how to set the table and to carry a plate of cucumbers for everyone to enjoy.

- Have him help me at the grocery store picking out fresh fruits and vegetables.

Oh gosh, now that I have started this list, I see I have been stomping out any attempts he has made toward becoming more independent.

Note from Vicki: When it became clear that Claire was ready to consider empowering Tyler with more responsibility in order to foster his independence, I showed her the Timeline for Training tool and she took off.

Step Four: Living with a Toddler

What can you do in the moment that will move the action forward without making things worse?

- Follow the plan I create
- When Tyler leaves the table the first time, remove his plate from the table
- Do not talk, remind, coax, or bribe
- Do not give in when he says he is hungry, but show respect for his choice to leave the table before he is done eating
- Remain firm and kind

Step Five: Raising an Adult

What character traits or life lessons can you teach in this situation that will benefit your child from age eighteen to eighty?

Resilience: I see a pattern now. Tyler falls apart and is unable to deal with many aspects of his life. He has these little meltdowns throughout the day, whether it is mealtime or a problem with what he is wearing, or whether we change plans or we are ending a playdate. He just doesn't have the resilience to overcome these difficult moments. I know from my own experience that to thrive as an adult you need to know you will recover from all sorts of difficulties. My job is to work with Tyler to develop this quality. I think this is more important to me than his actually eating his meal, because I now realize at the end of the day, he will eventually eat, but resilience? That's in a whole different league.

Self-control: I have been trying to control Tyler's tantrums instead of teaching him self-control, and I can see now that this character deficiency is impeding his ability to deal with many aspects of life. It is a trait that, once developed, will help him stay at the table even if he is done eating or refrain from screaming if he doesn't get what he wants. There are so many opportunities throughout our day together where I could be fostering this trait. Knowing the impact it will have on our lives today and on Tyler's life as an adult is all the motivation I need to stay with it. And, of course, it will help if his parents actually practice this same trait so he can see it in action.

Step Six: Creating an Intentional Plan

Describe the routine, structure, or plan you want to implement.

I wrote down some notes about what I wanted mealtime to look like and compared it with our current meal experience. I found that there is a huge discrepancy between what I was doing and what I wanted to be doing. Using my own creative genius I introduced the new system in the following way:

"Tyler, it's time for us to decide how we want to have meals together. The first thing we have to figure out is how we know whether someone wants to be eating or is done eating. Let's have a 'practice' meal now and see if we can figure it out together."

We sat down as a family for a "practice" meal and we talked and acted out behaviors that mimic someone who wants to eat and someone who is finished eating. Tyler thought it was hysterical that I was jumping up and down next to my chair and his dad was pretending to eat with his hands. He figured out quickly that these behaviors meant the person was done eating.

Then, we asked Tyler, "What does a person who wants to stay at the table for dinner look like?" He showed us someone sitting in a chair and someone eating pretend food with a fork and knife. Simple, two things a three-year-old can understand. So we said, "From now on, if you get up from the table or play with your food, that will tell us you are done with the meal. We will say, "Your actions are showing me that you're done with dinner. You may be excused and we will see you when we are done."

No wavering or waffling, no negotiating, pleading, threatening, or bribing, Just clear-cut expectations that, when not met, have clear-cut, reasonable, and respectful consequences.

Six weeks later: it has really been an effective way to help Tyler become more aware of his actions at dinner. My husband and I both realized that I would have to let go of the guilt of letting him go to bed hungry, because the alternative is neglecting my responsibility of teaching Tyler how to be a part of a group at mealtime. Tyler isn't always perfect at dinner, but he is only excused every once in a while these days. I realize that his level of self-control is increasing, which is spilling over into other areas of his life.

Step Seven: Trusting Your Intuition

What do you know about your child that will ensure you have set up a structure that will work for him?

Because he is only three years old, the only thing I am sure of is that Tyler needs practice recovering from his meltdowns, and the only way he can practice is if I follow through. I also know that he does much better when there are clear, consistent routines that we enforce with kindness and love.

School-Aged

Nicole is mom to eight-year-old Shannon and eleven-year-old Erin, and says:

We have two major challenges right now. Since we can't find a solution, every other area of life with the girls seems affected. Things are becoming so stressful that I have started complaining about the girls to other people. The first challenge is that the girls roll into the kitchen whenever they like, take things out of the pantry and fridge to make a snack, and when I come back to the kitchen it's a disaster. Food is left out and they don't bother to clean any of the mess up. They just leave it.

The second challenge is during mealtime. It's not unusual for them to complain about what I make (even though I tell them ahead of time what I'm making), come to the table with attitudes, fuss with the food, squabble with each other, and try to pick fights with Mike and me. Many nights they push the food around on their plates, then get up from the table in the middle of the meal and go into the kitchen to start making pasta or put a frozen pizza in the oven. This behavior is infuriating.

I have tried everything I can think of to get them to help with cleanup and to stay at the table and eat what I cook. I nag them, threaten them, scream at them, bang dishes around to try and make them feel guilty, and nothing works. Help!

Step One: Describing the Situation (in as few words as possible)

This is the result of the four questions you ask yourself to determine the mistaken goal of behavior.

Shannon and Erin are unwilling to clean up after they make a mess in the kitchen. They disrupt dinnertime and refuse to help pick up after the meal. I am **angry** at the way they treat me so I yell, lecture, threaten, and finally just throw in the towel and give up any hope that they will start helping. This tells me that the mistaken goal of their behavior is **power**.

Step Two: Developing a Relationship Blueprint

Identify any negative labels you use with your children that influence their self-ideal.

Without thinking about it, I have labeled my girls as disrespectful, sloppy, ungrateful, and selfish.

Replace the negative labels with positive attributes/qualities you want to use so your children develop a healthy self-ideal.

I want the girls to think of themselves as confident, consistent, dependable, cooperative, and appreciative. I can see that the girls are all of these things, but I don't focus my attention on these attributes. Instead, I focus on what they do that bugs me. Knowing that the labels we use with our kids create their self-ideal will make it much easier for me to break this habit of using negative labels when I am frustrated with them.

What parenting strategies do you use to manipulate your children into changing their behavior and what will you replace them with?

I shame them, blame them, and bully them. I already see some of this behavior showing up in their relationships with each other and their friends. It's a hard pill to swallow when I see that they learned to treat others this way from me, but I have to take responsibility for my choices and actions if I am going to ask the girls to do the same. Because they are older, I can think of many opportunities where I could include them in decision-making conversations, ask for their opinions, and teach them the skills for respectful conflict resolution. I think it would be helpful if we started to highlight how, even as a family, we have different styles and preferences and that we have created a way to support each of them. I don't think they realize that this is a real skill they could cultivate.

What qualities of a healthy relationship do you want to focus on that, over time, will influence or change this scenario in a positive way and support qualities found in a healthy relationship?

Appreciation: I'm starting with this because it's the one thing I haven't modeled for some time now. I rant at the girls to show me appreciation, but I am not giving it to them. I worked on an exercise with Vicki in which I share an appreciation with each of the girls each day around a quality they already possess but that I have overlooked, until they know without a doubt that I appreciate them. I know this will eventually influence their ability to show appreciation for me personally and for the life we are creating together as a family.

Step Three: Fostering Independence

Have you been supporting their independence in this area?

I haven't been supporting their independence in this area or any others. I just felt like they hit a certain age and should start helping more. They want more freedom and privileges and yet they don't want to help at home. When they refuse to help, I become angry and end up feeling powerless. It never dawned on me that I could start teaching them *how* to do things at a young age so that by the time they were eight and eleven they would have the skills and be excited at the prospect of more independence and responsibility. I complain that they are entitled, but what else would I expect? I fostered that attitude by waiting on them.

How will you foster your children's independence in a way that will influence this situation and ensure they are independent and self-sufficient when they are adults?

- Use the Timeline for Training to teach Shannon and Erin how to master self and home skills with ample time to practice without my pestering them.

- Agreements: this is a way for me to say, "I get where you're coming from and I'm willing to bend. Are you willing to agree to...?" It makes us feel like a team.
- Allow them a chance to make mistakes without barking at them.
- Give them more independence in the kitchen by involving them in meal planning and preparation.
- Follow through with our agreements around food, meals, and cleanup. For example, if they are not pleasant at dinner, then they are excused.
- Stop playing the maid and show them I have faith in their ability to learn to take care of themselves.
- No more nagging, lecturing, or threatening. When I feel the anger start to rise, I will leave the room and take deep breaths to calm down.

Step Four: Living with School-Aged Kids

What can you do in the moment that will move the action forward without making things worse?

- Do not engage in power struggles with my daughters. I will ask them when I would like help by offering them a choice and beginning the request, with "Would you be willing...?" This way they have the choice to answer yes or no.

- Remain calm and respectful in my actions and reactions.

- I will start to look at their privileges in terms of their ability to demonstrate their responsibilities. If they ask to go to a friend's house after school, I can reply, "Yes, as soon as you demonstrate that you will take care of your space and not contribute to more of a mess and more work for the other family members."

- Remain firm and kind.

- Follow through with agreements made around cleaning up after yourself and behavior at dinnertime. When we make agreements about dishes and keeping the kitchen clean and contributing to dinner and they ask me to help them with something, I will reply, "Yes, as soon as..."

Step Five: Raising an Adult

What character traits or life lessons can you teach in this situation that will benefit your child from age eighteen to eighty?

Self-sufficiency: I love my kids, but I don't want to be washing their dishes or balancing their checkbook for them in ten years when they are adults. I will put the time and effort into teaching them new and more difficult skills and then give them space to master the various things they need to know to be ready to leave in a few short years. I know firsthand how unhealthy it is to depend on other people because you lack the skills and the confidence to handle life's many demands. I do not want that for my kids.

Responsibility: The adult world expects that, as an adult, you will take full responsibility for your actions. No one is going to lecture my twenty-year-old kids about being responsible, and I realize now that lecturing and nagging are of no use to any of us. By doing things for them that they can do for themselves I undermine their ability to become responsible people. What they need is for me to show my faith in their abilities and to support them by creating structures and coming up with guidelines together.

Accountability: Accountability is another of those character traits that differentiates healthy from unhealthy adult behavior. Those of us willing to hold ourselves accountable to standards, values, or our choices typically live a more balanced and rewarding life. I can teach my kids about the importance of accountability by allowing them to make more decisions without my interference. My job is to develop the strength and faith to hold them accountable to the outcomes.

Step Six: Creating an Intentional Plan

Describe the routine, structure, or plan you want to implement.

1. The girls are allowed to make themselves three snacks a day as long as they clean up after themselves. The first time they leave a mess, the kitchen is closed to them until Monday morning. They can try again the following week.

2. The girls will help create the menu each week after the family meeting to ensure that there are meals that they enjoy and will eat.
3. The girls now have assigned tasks around every area of meal preparation and cleanup. This made it easier for them to stick with the job until the end.

Step Seven: Trusting Your Intuition

What do you know about your children that will ensure you have set up a structure that will work for them?

I know that Shannon is a grazer and it is really difficult for her to finish a big meal. I am going to take into consideration this particular idiosyncrasy. We can work together to plan snacks and meals that offer good options for her. Erin is a chatty kid who really wants to be in the center of the action, and I can use this personality trait to keep her engaged in meal preparation and cleanup. What a great time to visit, while we are working together at the sink.

CHAPTER SEVEN

Bring on the Bulldozer

Kids want bedrooms that are free from parental control and represent both their style and their preferences. Parents want bedrooms that are neat and organized and show that the child respects how hard their parents work to provide a comfortable home. The method is a sure way to balance out two very different perspectives and find common ground.

Toddlers

Sarah's three-year-old daughter, Lilly, loves to play! Her favorite activity is dumping all of her wooden blocks on the floor and building structures. Lilly loves to look at books and often makes her way through her entire bookshelf. She also gets a kick out of pulling all of her clothes out of her closet. Mom explains:

The problem is, when it's time to clean up she just yells, "No!" over and over! That seems to be her favorite word lately, and it's driving me nuts. I recently had another baby, and I just don't have the patience for this. I try everything to encourage and include her in the cleanup. I sing the cleanup song, I say the ABCs, and I even count. Nothing seems to work so I end up frustrated and annoyed, and fall back on giving her a time-out. She continues playing while I clean up and I end up feeling resentful. I end up in a power struggle with a three-year-old, which, ultimately, she wins. How can I make her clean up after herself?

Step One: Describing the Situation (in as few words as possible)

This is the result of the four questions you ask yourself to determine the mistaken goal of behavior.

My daughter takes books off the shelf, empties clothes out of drawers, and dumps bins of toys all over her room. When asked to pick them us she screams, "No!" I try to **engage her** in the pickup by singing songs and other entertaining tactics. When that doesn't work I lose my cool and resort to **yelling or punishing her.** This tells me the mistaken goals of her behavior are **attention and power.**

> **Note from Vicki:** Sometimes, as children become more discouraged, their behavior deteriorates. They start with attention as their goal and end with power as their goal. Remember, you can reverse this downward spiral by making one small shift in your parenting.

Step Two: Developing a Relationship Blueprint

Identify any negative labels you use with your children that influence their self-ideal.

I often think of my daughter as demanding, defiant, and overly dramatic.

Replace the negative labels with positive attributes/qualities you want to use so your children develop a healthy self-ideal.

I want my daughter to be patient, organized, thoughtful, and cooperative. I know Lilly is young and I fell into the same pattern many of my friends did in thinking that our kids were too young to be influenced by the way we described them. Now I understand on a deep level that the labels your parents use to describe you are the ones you carry with you your entire life. It's true that Lilly has a lot of growing to do before she embodies these positive attributes, and there is nothing more important than to feed her emotional health by describing her in these positive ways.

What parenting strategies do you use to manipulate your children into changing their behavior and what will you replace them with?

I spend hours entertaining her and making everything fun and easy or I become easily frustrated (because I am exhausted) and resort to time-outs and shaming her. These are two parenting extremes that don't work to bring about any kind of cooperation between us or offer a solution that works beyond the moment. If I want Lilly to enter into satisfying relationships with other people, she has to learn a number of strategies and she has to learn them from our interactions. It makes giving up what I have been doing much more appealing. I know one of the strategies I will initiate immediately is walking away when I get upset.

What qualities of a healthy relationship do you want to focus on that, over time, will influence or change this scenario in a positive way and support qualities found in a healthy relationship?

There are two words I use with Lilly throughout the day that I have to work on. "Cooperation," which until now meant, please do what I want you to do and don't give me any crap. I know the way to build cooperation is to include Lilly more and I can start with choices and grow from there. "Understanding" because I ask Lilly to understand when I am grouchy or short or distracted, but I don't show her the same courtesy. I will use the word in sentences that show Lilly that I understand when she is frustrated, upset, or having a hard time transitioning.

Step Three: Fostering Independence

Have you been supporting her independence in this area?

No, not at all. I do things for Lilly because it is easier and faster and I can do what I want. I now understand this is totally indulgent and selfish on my part.

How will you foster your child's independence in a way that will influence this situation and ensure she is independent and self-sufficient when she is an adult?

Fostering Lilly's independence will take some juggling. I can be an all-or-nothing kind of gal and I can imagine I will pile too much on her too quickly. If she isn't able to master the skill immediately, I imagine myself jumping back in and taking it over. I know from reading *Duct Tape Parenting* that there is an exercise for evaluating where your kids are on a continuum of tasks, the Timeline for Training, and if I use that as a guideline I think I can balance my all-or-nothing attitude and create a system for fostering Lilly's independence without overwhelming her. I'm going to start with self skills and go from there.

Step Four: Living with a Toddler

What can you do in the moment that will move the action forward without making things worse?

- Do not fight with a three-year-old under any circumstances.
- Ignore her screams. She is angry, not hurt.
- Remain calm and consistent. Follow through with my words.
- Leave the room if I can't control my own behavior.

Step Five: Raising an Adult

What character traits or life lessons can you teach in this situation that will benefit your child from age eighteen to eighty?

Balance: I want Lilly to know how to balance her life, so that she can attend to all the different areas of it, like her work, partner, kids, friends, interests, and herself. This is a character trait I was introduced to late in my life and it continues to be a struggle for me. What does Vicki say, you can't give your kids something you don't have yourself? This is a perfect example of what she is talking about.

Living a balanced life means staying present and living in the moment, so that you can organize your time and enjoy your commitments. By staying present with Lilly and enjoying the moment, we will be learning to live our lives in balance together.

Step Six: Creating an Intentional Plan

Describe the routine, structure, or plan you want to implement.

I started to understand that the systems and routines that were working pre-baby were no longer going to work for a number of reasons, the least of which is that I am less patient and I have less energy by the end of the day.

- Minimize the number of toys. Lilly has too many options and it is over-whelming. Not only in choosing what to play with, but having so many toys to clean up.
- I began using the phrase "As soon as..." For example, Lilly moves on from an activity and I notice that she did not clean up. She comes to me and asks me for a hug, a drink of water, or to read her a book. My answer is "Yes! As soon as you clean up the toys you were just playing with."
- I model for Lilly what taking out and putting away toys looks like. No talking on and on, just showing, and it is making a huge difference.

Step Seven: Trusting Your Intuition

What do you know about your child that will ensure you have set up a structure that will work for her?

I know that my daughter responds more reasonably and pleasantly when she sees me modeling qualities. I know that she feels more secure when there are routines that are consistent and reasonable. I can provide this for Lilly and I am excited at the prospect of our relationship growing over the years.

Teens

James, a single parent, shares that his teenage son Grant refuses to clean his room whether he tries enticements or punishments. He is at a loss and is worried that if things don't turn around quickly, their entire relationship will be in jeopardy.

My teenage son's room is a disaster area. Grant is fourteen years old and is perfectly capable of cleaning it, but he refuses to do so. I have to threaten to take his video games away in order to get him to clean it before his grandparents come to visit! I'm also fed up with doing his laundry and leaving it on his bed ready to be put away, only to find it scattered all over his floor mixed in with dirty laundry (dirty laundry that he has *not* brought to the laundry room). I've told him many times that I refuse to be his maid and something needs to change. He cleans his room eventually, but only when I resort to yelling, threatening, and ranting. Otherwise, the room is a pit.

Step One: Describing the Situation (in as few words as possible)

This is the result of the four questions you ask yourself to determine the mistaken goal of behavior.

My fourteen-year-old refuses to clean his room or put his laundry away unless I threaten him with the loss of a privilege. I am really **disappointed and a bit hurt** that a bright kid who is afforded all kinds of opportunities refuses to take care of this one thing. This tells me that his mistaken goal of behavior is **revenge.**

Step Two: Developing a Relationship Blueprint

Identify any negative labels you use with your children that influence their self-ideal.

It's easy for me to think of my son as lazy, self-indulgent, and inconsiderate when I feel hurt, which seems like all the time.

Replace the negative labels with positive attributes/qualities you want to use so your children develop a healthy self-ideal.

Helpful, organized, cooperative, kind, and family oriented are qualities I'd like to help my son cultivate. I don't want to admit it, but the last few years I have taken Grant's unwillingness to cooperate with me personally, and as a result I am lashing out at him. I can think of so many occasions where he demonstrates his helpful nature: the way he organizes important assignments, cooperates with friends and coaches, shows kindness to other kids and his aging grandparents, and makes time for family when they come to visit, but I don't comment. I think I came to believe that unless Grant was "perfect," I wasn't going to verbalize anything positive I noticed about him. I was being a child when I am supposed to be a parent raising a future adult.

What parenting strategies do you use to manipulate your children into changing their behavior and what will you replace them with?

I threaten him, overpower him, and belittle him. I felt true embarrassment and shame when I finished this exercise. I would be appalled if my son ever treated anyone in this manner, so I am taking responsibility for my behavior and making course corrections immediately. The truth is, I could see Grant giving in to other people who bully him like I did more than I can see him inflicting this kind of emotional pain on anyone else. In either case, it wouldn't constitute a healthy relationship. Every parent could benefit from answering these three simple questions. It is a true indication of why the relationship with our kids might be suffering or strained and what we can do to turn things around immediately, if we have the courage.

What qualities of a healthy relationship do you want to focus on that, over time, will influence or change this scenario in a positive way and support qualities found in a healthy relationship?

Personal responsibility: I have been a complete hypocrite in this area. I don't take personal responsibility for my words, my attitude, or my actions, but I demand it of not only Grant but other people in my life. I can see that now. My tendency is to blame other people for my bad mood or to justify my nasty attitude when I am stressed. I don't ever say, "Yeah, I'm tired and stressed and I'm being a jerk and I'm sorry." It's a hard pill to swallow, but it's true. I'll be spending more time modeling this character trait and less time demanding it of others, especially of my son.

Step Three: Fostering Independence

Have you been supporting his independence in this area?

I realize now that I have been doing anything but fostering his independence. I have been treating him like he is "less than," not only by doing things for him but also by criticizing and shaming him for the way he ends up doing things. I had no idea I was causing this rift in our relationship, to the extent that my own child didn't feel safe coming to me when he made a mistake with the laundry.

How will you foster your child's independence in a way that will influence this situation and ensure he is independent and self-sufficient when he is an adult?

- Use the Timeline for Training. It's time for me to sit down and assess Grant's skill levels and start teaching him about not only laundry but budgeting, cooking, how to schedule an oil change for the car, and so on. The list is long and I have a feeling he has been waiting for me to invite him into this process.
- Show faith. I can encourage him to take on a more active role in the decision-making process concerning family policies. Things like curfews, which sports he wants to play, where we go on vacation, how to handle cell phone issues. I have been a complete dictator so he hasn't had a chance to develop much independence in this area.
- Show him respect by giving him space and support. I think the biggest shift I have to make in order to support his independence is to stop peppering him with intrusive questions. I want to know everything and I can get hurtful if Grant seems evasive with me. I owe him an apology and I will have to not only take personal responsibility for my disrespectful behavior, I will also have to ask Grant to collaborate with me on ways to temper my desire to know every detail of his life.

Step Four: Living with a Teen

What can you do in the moment that will move the action forward without making things worse?

I won't be going into Grant's room without an invitation from him, and he has willingly accepted his laundry responsibility, so there is truly no reason for me to get involved in this area of his life any longer. Problem solved.

What I will do is be on the lookout for other areas where I might insert myself and instead keep my mouth shut. (This means I may have to buy another roll or two of duct tape.) If I give myself time to think and remember that collaborating and taking personal responsibility are values I want to model, I will be able to stay calm and keep things in perspective.

Step Five: Raising an Adult

What character traits or life lessons can you teach in this situation that would benefit your child from age eighteen to eighty?

Self-reliance: I realize now that not fostering my son's independence and failing to give him time to master self, social, and life skills has damaged his confidence. He spends his energy either resisting my attempts to manage his life or avoiding the things he doesn't think he can handle. I know how important it is to trust yourself, to know that you can handle life and that you are capable of solving problems, so I have a lot of work ahead of me. Grant doesn't have much faith in his own abilities right now, so I have my work cut out for me.

Open communication: I can't help but think that if our relationship had been different, Grant would have been able to come to me and express his feelings and let me know how I was hurting him. Communication is crucial in any relationship. And it goes well beyond just talking about your day. And if the other aspects of the relationship are fractured, then open communication is difficult if not impossible. Our lines of communication are wide open (now) and I feel confident that this will trickle into other relationships in both of our lives.

Step Six: Creating an Intentional Plan

Describe the routine, structure, or plan you want to implement.

The room:

- Do not enter without knocking first.
- Wait for an invitation to come in.
- When I do come in, I have been asked not to comment on the state of the room.

I can do all of this, because I am practicing and modeling personal responsibility, which is part of my relationship blueprint.

The laundry: After I taught Grant how to do the laundry it was no longer an issue. We decided that if his clothes weren't taken care of he would have to take on the responsibility of buying his own clothes. This made sense to Grant, and although we have revisited this issue a few times, he has nearly mastered not just doing the laundry but organizing his day so he has time to do it. He is learning time management and day-planning skills at the same time he is learning to do laundry.

Step Seven: Trusting Your Intuition

What do you know about your child that will ensure you have set up a structure that will work for him?

I know that Grant is a private person by nature. He is quiet and content with his own company. He doesn't take up much psychic space. Giving him space, talking with him when I am calm and thoughtful, asking for his thoughts and opinions, and accepting that he just doesn't want to answer all my questions makes it easier for me to not take things personally and to maximize our time together by talking about things that matter. When I teach Grant new skills, it is best if I follow his lead and then allow him plenty of time to practice without comment; otherwise, he shuts down. He is a kind and sensitive young man who demonstrates his maturity by not only putting up with me, but accepting me for who I am.

CHAPTER EIGHT

Morning Meltdowns

Perhaps the most universal struggle in families today is the morning routine where both parent and child are reduced to tears and tantrums. With some advance preparation, a shift in attitude, and a family who is working from the same playbook, you can smooth out the morning madness once-and-for-all.

Toddlers

Jill is mom to three-year-old Caitlin, and says:

I have a three-year-old who just started going to preschool two mornings a week. She seems to be enjoying herself and it's great for me to have some time to get things done, but our mornings have become very complicated. She insists on being carried up and down the stairs, and if I refuse she throws a temper tantrum that I just don't have time for. Getting dressed can be smooth as long as I'm there and giving her lots of praise for being a big girl. She's a mischievous one, though, and when I try to sneak away to get myself dressed or have a quick cup of coffee before we walk out the door, she ends up taking off the outfit that I have picked out! By the time I get her ready again, she is completely unreasonable and grumpy. Luckily, the preschool is only a few minutes from our house, but we are still late every day by at least twenty minutes. I end up frustrated and huffy on our drive and she refuses to get out of the car even though I know she absolutely loves being at school. It's a mess. She is really challenging and I have no idea how to make our mornings run more peacefully.

Step One: Describing the Situation (in as few words as possible)

This is the result of the four questions you ask yourself to determine the mistaken goal of behavior.

I am feeling **challenged** and a bit miffed at my three-year-old's behavior, especially when we are getting ready in the morning. Caitlin demands I help and refuses to cooperate or do anything independently. Not wanting to get into a full-blown power struggle, I end up giving in to Caitlin's demands just so we can get out the door. This tells me that her mistaken goal of behavior is **power**.

Step Two: Developing a Relationship Blueprint

Identify any negative labels you use with your children that influence their self-ideal.

I notice that when I describe my mornings with Caitlin I label her as demanding, unreasonable, stubborn, sneaky, and snotty.

Replace the negative labels with positive attributes/qualities you want to use so your children develop a healthy self-ideal.

Understanding, supportive, flexible, compassionate, and forgiving are the positive qualities I want my daughter to develop. Alright, I know she is young and she probably hasn't demonstrated any of these attributes as of yet, but if I start focusing on them now I can train myself to be on the lookout for them. And if I notice and appreciate them when they do show up and I model them for her, I can be a real influence in how this little girl sees herself and the kinds of people she is drawn to. Becoming an influencer rather than a dictator in my child's life is exciting and invigorating.

What parenting strategies do you use to manipulate your children into changing their behavior and what will you replace them with?

Initially I give in, which is teaching Caitlin that she can bully people into doing what she wants if she is nasty enough. This isn't going to work with anyone but her mother so it has to stop immediately. I had to really search for what else I do that is unhealthy and I realized that I withhold my affection from her when she has challenged me to the point that I feel out of control. It's my way of getting back at her, at making her suffer a little bit. I can't believe I am admitting this, but if I don't confront this now and change the way I interact with my daughter I am going to have to accept that any difficulties she has in her adult relationships will be the result of the way I parented her. The stakes are just too high for me to be in denial. Giving her choices, redirecting her, teaching her how to accept her frustration and move through it, showing her how patient I can be so that she models my behavior and walking away when I reach my limit are all strategies that will work in the adult world.

What qualities of a healthy relationship do you want to focus on that, over time, will influence or change this scenario in a positive way and support qualities found in a healthy relationship?

Confidence and conviction are the words I will focus on over the next few months. I seem to lack both of these when it comes to making parenting decisions and I think it's influencing some of my interactions with Caitlin. I have to consider my parenting options, create a plan, and stand behind the plan even if it means Caitlin is upset. Connecting what I am doing now with the kind of woman Caitlin will become makes it easier to hold myself accountable.

Understanding: I knew that starting preschool might be hard on Caitlin, yet I let myself be fooled by how much she seemed to like it. I didn't connect her behavior at home in the mornings before school to the fact that she is actually still transitioning and getting used to this new routine. I want to give her more understanding around that and have more patience in this situation because of the circumstances. As an adult woman who has gone through some transitional life changes myself, I know how important it is to show yourself some understanding through the struggle and to surround yourself with friends who understand what you are going through. I want Caitlin to be sensitive to other people and what's happening in their lives. We don't always know the backstory, but this can significantly affect behavior and the decisions people make.

Cooperation: Until I worked with Vicki, it never dawned on me to think about what it takes for a person to be willing to cooperate with another person. Vicki asked me if I would be more likely to cooperate with Person A, someone who treated me in a kind, respectful, and appreciative way, or Person B, someone who was rude, demanding, and impatient. When Vicki put it that way, I got it. Of course I would be more willing to cooperate with Person A. But all this time, I was expecting and demanding cooperation from Caitlin rather than earning the right to ask for it. Obviously, from an adult perspective, you are going to have real trouble in both your professional and personal relationships if you cannot or are unwilling to cooperate with others.

Mutual respect: I never thought about the need to "respect" my three-year-old. I had certainly considered the need to be loving and nurturing, but respect is not something I had considered until this exercise. What is going on with Caitlin and me and the constant power struggles has so much to do with a lack of respect on my part. Don't get me wrong, I sing, read to her, play with her, give her lots of love and attention, but I don't respect her wants and preferences. I was not looking at this little girl as a future adult in the making, I was looking at her like a stubborn, demanding, and unreasonable three-year-old. (Ha, that could be me on any day.) The most fascinating part of this particular character trait is that it starts with the word mutual, which has really been missing in our relationship.

Step Three: Fostering Independence

Have you been supporting her independence in this area?

I thought I was supporting her independence by making her walk up the stairs alone or sitting and praising her while she dressed herself, but that was not supporting independence. Praising her was actually creating the opposite effect. I was treating her like she either couldn't do certain things or making her think she needed me and my praise in order to do them. She is a capable little monkey and needs me to give her more space. That being said, I need to find the balance between giving her space to do things on her own and still being available to her emotionally while she deals with the newness of school and being away from me for a few hours a week. While I will make changes to encourage her independence, I will also make more efforts to connect with her and try to understand her temperament during the day and why she might be a bit more sensitive or needy at times.

Step Four: Living with a Toddler

What can you do in the moment that will move the action forward without making things worse?

I have been starting the mornings anticipating the struggles that will come with Caitlin. She could probably sense this and she met my expectations. My whole attitude needs to change.

- Remain consistent with routines.
- Stay calm, firm, and kind.
- Keep moving. I will go ahead and get myself ready, trust the systems we have in place, and show her with my actions and energy that I will not engage in a power struggle.

Step Five: Raising an Adult

What character traits or life lessons can you teach in this situation that would benefit your child from age eighteen to eighty?

Perseverance: I know that Caitlin will come across situations in her life as a child (getting that other leg in her pants or getting her shirt over her head) that challenge and frustrate her. I am certain that she will be faced with daily challenges as an adult. She needs the remaining fifteen years with us to practice sticking with things that are hard. As a mother, it's hard to watch your child struggle, but knowing that I am supporting a character trait that will serve her well as an adult helps me keep my eye on the prize.

Patience: I say that I want Caitlin to persevere and develop a "stick with it" attitude, and I also know that along with that character trait comes the need for big doses of patience. Change doesn't happen overnight. We don't master a new skill the second time we try it. (Gee, I wonder who in Caitlin's life she will learn patience from, because neither of her parents demonstrates much patience with any part of their lives.) We have both been called impatient by our friends and colleagues, and I am guessing that, without knowing it, we have been putting pressure on Caitlin. This might explain some of her edginess.

Step Six: Creating an Intentional Plan

Describe the routine, structure, or plan you want to implement.

- Use the Timeline for Training: take the time to train Caitlin on some self-care tasks, so that she will have more ownership over her own routine.
- For the time being, I will not expect to get out of the door on time and I will accept that. Working on Caitlin's training and a mutually respectful relationship will be my priority over arriving someplace on time. This is Caitlin's emotional health at stake. If she were physically ill, I would miss work without hesitation.
- Offer more choices (specifically around clothing) and then move out of the way. This will show her that I have faith in her ability to get herself dressed and I am close by if she gets stumped.
- Stop the praising.
- Stay calm and consistent. If she demands to be carried up the stairs the answer is the same each morning: "Caitlin, I trust that you can walk up the stairs on your own." If she chooses to stay at the bottom of the stairs and scream, I will go about my business of getting ready and while I'm up there I might call her up to show her something (redirect) or ask her for her help opening my toothpaste (ask her for help).
- Ask, "Would you be willing to...?" instead of telling her exactly what to do.

Step Seven: Trusting Your Intuition

What do you know about your child that will ensure you have set up a structure that will work for her?

Caitlin is an inquisitive kid, and I am wondering now if part of what she is experimenting with is the cause and effect of life. If I think about other situations, I can see clearly that Caitlin is interested in understanding how things work, including toasters and ignitions. She is trying to find the answer to "If I do this, what will happen? If I do that, what will happen?" If she is trying to understand her world, I could engage her with questions like "What will happen if you...?" This will open up a whole new way for us to connect and to cooperate with each other.

Note from Vicki: Jill reported back that once she began using the question "What will happen if you...?" the dynamic changed dramatically with Caitlin. Many of the daily challenges turned into simple exploratory sessions. Jill says, "Caitlin would demand I carry her up the stairs and if I didn't she would scream and throw a temper tantrum. Initially, I decided to just leave her there to scream and go about my morning. But then, using the 'What do you know about your child?' question as a jumping off point, I tried this: 'Caitlin, what would happen if you tried to do cartwheels up the stairs?' You could hear a pin drop. She thought about it, lined her body up to do one, then looked at me and said, 'That won't work; walking works best,' and up she came. Problem solved. It's happened on a number of occasions with other things and we have side-stepped another power struggle altogether. Knowing this about Caitlin is going to make our lives together so much more delicious."

School-Aged

Gabe says:

My ten-year-old son refuses to get out of bed in the morning. I hear him hit snooze at least five times and I am in and out of his room trying to drag him out of bed. It is totally disruptive to the rest of the family because it causes me so much stress while I'm trying to get out the door for work. By the time he gets up and is finally ready, he has missed his ride to school and barely has time to grab a piece of toast. I end up having to drive him myself, lecture him the whole way to school, and show up to work late.

Step One: Describing the Situation (in as few words as possible)

This is the result of the four questions you ask yourself to determine the mistaken goal of behavior.

My ten-year-old son, Brad, refuses to get himself out of bed on time in the morning. I feel **frustrated** and **helpless** and have no idea how to get through to him. I end up packing his lunch, packing his backpack, and driving him to school, and then I'm late for work. This tells me that his mistaken goal of behavior is **avoidance.**

Step Two: Developing a Relationship Blueprint

Identify any negative labels you use with your children that influence their self-ideal.

I have labeled my child as insensitive, immature, unmotivated, scatterbrained, and disconnected.

Replace the negative labels with positive attributes/qualities you want to use so your children develop a healthy self-ideal.

Engaged, courageous, honest, and respectful are just a few of the attributes I want my son to use when he describes himself. I know that if he sees himself in these terms, he will look for others who embody these qualities and attributes. If I am honest, I know he already has some of these qualities, but I haven't done a good job supporting and acknowledging them. Here is my big "aha." I tried to avoid doing this exercise because I suspected that I would learn more about myself than my son, and that is exactly what happened. If I want my son to be engaged in the world, embodying a man who has the courage to admit his mistakes and apologize when necessary, I am going to have to start modeling that behavior for him.

What parenting strategies do you use to manipulate your children into changing their behavior and what will you replace them with?

I give up and then I place the blame on Brad. I think I talk to him like he is a toddler instead of a boy who is entering puberty, which further fractures our relationship and gets him to withdraw. I have sole custody of the kids after a very difficult and hurtful divorce, and if I take that into consideration I think Brad might need me to reconnect with him in a new way, which I haven't taken the time to do. This means revamping my parenting approach and including Brad in conversations, so he learns what strategies to use in his adult relationships to work through difficult times or misunderstandings.

I also learned that I have modeled for Brad that if something is difficult, there are any number of ways to avoid dealing with it, and I think this is at the root of our current challenge around the morning routine. Our communication needs work and, as a father, it is my responsibility to start focusing my attention on these positive attributes, so my son can see himself in this positive light.

What qualities of a healthy relationship do you want to focus on that, over time, will influence or change this scenario in a positive way and support qualities found in a healthy relationship?

Courage: As I said earlier, I have to start modeling courage, and that means admitting my mistakes, dealing with things I would rather avoid, and accepting that I am not the best at everything and that it is difficult for me to talk about subjects that bring up strong emotions. If I can really show my son what it is like to be a courageous person, I know it will serve him throughout his life.

Respect: I accuse Brad of being disrespectful and demand he show me respect. There it is, I demand that he show me respect. I am working on a bulleted list of all the ways I can show my son and myself the true meaning of the word respect.

Note from Vicki: This exercise drove home the importance of the relationship blueprint. Having just come through a painful divorce, Gabe had lost sight of the joy relationships can be if one commits to open, honest, and respectful communication as part of daily life.

Step Three: Fostering Independence

Have you been supporting his independence in this area?

My idea of fostering independence was to tell my kids what they should do and how they should do it. I had an expectation that they would do it just as I wanted every damn time. What a jerk. Therefore the answer to this question is—no. I have not been supporting or fostering independence, especially Brad's.

How will you foster your child's independence in a way that will influence this situation and ensure he is independent and self-sufficient when he is an adult?

- Talk to Brad about how he wants to get himself up in the morning and, if he isn't going to get up, how he will get to school without me.

- Talk to Brad about all the other areas he would like me to back out of and then make sure he knows how to take care of them.
- Think ahead to what he will need to know how to do as a teenager, and stay one step ahead of him.

Step Four: Living with a School-Aged Child

What can you do in the moment that will move the action forward without making things worse?

When I look back on this last school year, I realize that I had been on top of Brad since the very first day of school. I was so worried that things would fall apart after the divorce. I was awarded full custody of the kids, and I was hypervigilant in making sure he was up on time, had everything he needed, did his homework, and got involved in sports and other activities outside of school. Now I can see that I jumped in before even giving him a chance to figure a few things out on his own. I will:

- Decide what I will do and respect what he decides to do, even if that means he sleeps through the alarm clock. I have to trust that he will figure out how to get to school another way or that a few days of being late and stressed will be all the motivation this kid needs to get up at the first bell.

- Send the message to him that I won't be upset or disappointed in him if he messes up. This supports those earlier relationship traits I talked about.

Step Five: Raising an Adult

What character traits or life lessons can you teach in this situation that will benefit your child from age eighteen to eighty?

Independence: It just never occurred to me that in order for Brad to become independent, he needed me to provide opportunities for him to practice on his own. His mother doted on him when he was younger and then when he started spending the majority of his time with me, I did things for him so that my life would be easier. He never had a chance to find out what he could do or a chance to practice and improve. No wonder he avoids trying new and difficult things.

Responsibility: Along with independence comes responsibility, and I know that the adults who take responsibility for their decisions and actions have a much better experience as adults. In order for Brad to take more responsibility for himself I have to step out of the way and allow that to happen. It is going to be messy from time to time, but that is what parenting is all about—being there for the messes and talking with your kids so they can benefit from all the learning. Instead of feeling anxious, I am actually beginning to feel a new calm. I can do this. I understand how important these character traits are in creating a healthy adult life and I want my kids to have the opportunity to develop these traits.

Step Six: Creating an Intentional Plan

Describe the routine, structure, or plan you want to implement.

Family meetings: When I learned about family meetings my initial thought was, "Okay, if you say so, Vicki." But truthfully, it didn't sound like something that would make a difference for our family or for Brad and me specifically. I should have known that Vicki wouldn't recommend a strategy if she didn't think it would make a substantial difference in our family dynamic, and this time was no different—it did. All four elements of the family meeting are powerful, relevant, and support everything on my relationship blueprint and the character traits I want my adult children to embody.

No more interfering: Once I apologized to Brad for getting in his way and trying to take over with something that he is perfectly capable of managing, we put new systems in place.

- He can snooze as many times as he chooses. He asked if I could come in at 7:15 and give him the same quick "neck nuzzle" I gave him when he was younger, while he gets used to this new routine. Of course I said I would. He will choose to wake up at that time or keep on snoozing. At some point I plan to remove my morning visit and leave it completely for him to manage, but for now this feels like a great compromise and certainly a step in the right direction.

- He will be out of the door on time for school with or without his gear and with or without food in his belly.

- If he misses his ride I will not drive him, as it will make me late for work. It is then up to him to call the school to let them know that he will be late and to find alternate transportation. He will be in touch with me to let me know when he arrives safely at school.

- Any consequences that arise from tardiness at school are up to him to work out with school administration. I will not sign any of his tardies "excused."

Encouragement: Vicki says to "encourage, encourage, encourage," and that is what I am doing. I used to think that encouragement sounded similar to praising, but I was mistaken. I'm noticing his attempts, commenting on his progress and improvement, focusing on his strengths, and, most importantly, I am learning to show faith in him. Since I have started to encourage him, I notice that he is finding the courage to talk more openly with me and to take responsibility when he messes up and oversleeps, and with this new courage comes a new attitude about life in general.

Step Seven: Trusting Your Intuition

What do you know about your child that will ensure you have set up a structure that will work for him?

I have a lot to learn about Brad. He has been hiding himself away, so it's hard for me to really know how to support his true nature. We have started talking about redesigning his entire schedule and his routines to support the unique human being he is, and this new plan is helping. It looks like I might be living with a night owl, and if that's the case, it would explain a lot about why he struggles in the morning. I also know that he is sensitive to criticism and does not want to disappoint the people he loves and admires. Taking this into consideration whenever I communicate with Brad helps us work together to find ways to give each other feedback that is helpful instead of hurtful.

CHAPTER NINE

Containing the Chaos

We all know kids are messy, but do they have to spread the mess throughout the house? They do if there is no system in place to make the cleanup smoother and more consistent and if the messages they receive when they do try to help undermine their feelings of acceptance and competency.

Toddlers

Jane is mom to four-year-old Brendan, and says:

My child is a Tasmanian devil. It was actually really cute when he was smaller. He has always been into everything and is so curious and interested in exploring everything he can get his hands on. Now that he is four years old, it's become old. I feel like I spend my life following him around cleaning up his messes and putting out fires, so to speak. I love his love of learning and playing, and I don't want to interfere with that by making him stop what he is focusing on to clean up a mess from his last project, but by five o'clock at night my house is a disaster area and I'm left cleaning it all up, because he simply refuses to help. If I'm ever feeling brave enough to push the issue of cleanup with him by counting, threatening, or giving him a time-out, the situation just seems to escalate. More recently, he is becoming aggressive: pushing past me to get out of the room, screaming in my face, and calling me names. Now that he's a little older, there seems to be extra sass that goes along with it all. He really needs to start taking care of his things and cleaning up after himself and also needs to know who's really in charge around here. *Me.*"

Step One: Describing the Situation (in as few words as possible)

This is the result of the four questions you ask yourself to determine the mistaken goal of behavior.

My four-year-old pulls out every toy, empties the Tupperware drawers and the pantry, takes the blender apart, and then walks away from the carnage. He refuses to clean up and is becoming aggressive with me when I ask him to pick up behind himself. **I am angry**. I feel like my control as a parent is being threatened. I am ashamed to say it, but I am baffled and completely confused by his behavior and overall attitude. This tells me the mistaken goal of his behavior is **power**.

Step Two: Developing a Relationship Blueprint

Identify any negative labels you use with your children that influence their self-ideal.

When I focus on feeling out of control with my child I use labels like Tasmanian devil, explosive, aggressive, and mean.

Replace the negative labels with positive attributes/qualities you want to use so your children develop a healthy self-ideal.

I want to replace the negative labels with independent, resourceful, and compassionate. Yes, this is how I want my son to see himself and if I don't start using those words in his presence and looking for opportunities to point out when he is demonstrating them, he isn't going to have a good foundation for building a healthy self-ideal. I want to create a working list that has all the qualities I hope my child embodies, so I remember how important it is to constantly remind him of the remarkable person he is becoming.

What parenting strategies do you use to manipulate your children into changing their behavior and what will you replace them with?

It is a battle of wills with the two of us. I try and overpower him in whatever way seems legitimate at the time. Obviously, none of them works, but I am teaching him a lot about how two people in a relationship interact with each other, and it isn't good. The more I try to overpower him, the more he tries to overpower me. The list of options that Vicki provided gives me hope that with time, practice, and patience, I will be able to incorporate more of them into my parenting and steer clear of the disrespectful and hurtful ways I deal with my strong-willed child.

What qualities of a healthy relationship do you want to focus on that, over time, will influence or change this scenario in a positive way and support qualities found in a healthy relationship?

Cooperation: I tried for more than five years to become a mom. I believe this is partly why I am having trouble admitting that Brendan is no longer a baby and is capable of doing a lot more for himself than I give him credit for. I haven't been cooperating with his desire to do more for himself and to have more of a voice in his own life, like the clothes he wears, that he would rather take a shower than a bath, that he doesn't want to cuddle in bed like he used to, or what he wants for dinner. I just make decisions for him and don't look back. I know I want to start inviting Brendan to be a more active participant in the family and include him in the majority of the decisions that concern him.

Respect: In a nutshell, I have to respect that Brendan is a human being, not my possession. He is not mine, but I was treating him like he was, and that is the most disrespectful thing I could do. This belief was influencing every single one of my parenting decisions and I was giving myself permission to be a tyrant in his life. I think I can start to show him respect by allowing him to be more autonomous and independent, and it will grow from there.

Step Three: Fostering Independence

Have you been supporting your child's independence in this area?

No, not even a little bit. I realized that all the pushback around cleaning up wasn't really about cleaning up at all. This pushback was actually his way of yelling, "Mom, I can do more than pick up the stupid toys!" He wanted to be asked to do more important things, and once I finally realized that, everything changed.

How will you foster your child's independence in a way that will influence this situation and ensure he is independent and self-sufficient when he is an adult?

- Stop resorting to punishments, time-outs, threats, and other disrespectful actions that don't work in the long term and also hurt the relationship. When I realized how much of our day was spent in power struggles, I made it my mission to back off.

- Invite Brendan to help with "adult" tasks around the house and let him know that his help makes a difference.

- Use family meetings and contributions: Giving him a job/responsibility every day ended up showing me how willing he actually is to help pick up, because he *feels* useful, helpful, and needed.

- Continue retraining myself and my thought process. It's a work in process, but I'm willing to keep my eyes and ears open and pay more attention to what my son is actually telling me with his behaviors. I believe that through this practice, his sense of self-esteem and self-worth will improve because he is feeling that he plays an important role in the success of our family.

Step Four: Living with a Toddler

What can you do in the moment that will move the action forward without making things worse?

- Ask, "Would you be willing to clean up those Legos?" and, if the answer is no, ask him "What would you be willing to do?" I know that sometimes the answer just might be no, but it's respectful for me to ask him instead of demanding that he do it. This takes the element of power out of it for me and it lets him know that he is at choice and so am I. I might choose to pick up and put things away in a closet where they aren't available for him when he goes looking the next day. I might choose to leave the mess out. It will depend on the situation.

- Stop manipulating and threatening. If I do choose to put his toys away, I will just do it and not use this action as a threat to try to coerce him into putting his toys away out of fear that he will lose them.

Step Five: Raising an Adult

What character traits or life lessons can you teach in this situation that will benefit your child from age eighteen to eighty?

I want my little guy to grow up with the self-confidence it takes to go out and conquer his world, the self-discipline it takes to do things you don't want to do, and the compassion to honor himself for the one-of-a-kind person that he is.

Self-confidence: Vicki tells us all the time that self-confidence comes from doing, not from the lip service parents pay their kids, so I have got to make sure I don't try to make life easy for Brendan. And, I have to follow through on what I say so he has the confidence that he can move past the difficult moments in life. And, at four years old, that means picking up your toys even when you don't want to.

Self-discipline: By yelling at Brendan or picking up the toys for him, I have totally neglected to introduce him to the idea that it takes self-discipline to do things you don't want to do. I am going to have to take the time to teach him how to do things, but then support that learning with patience. I am also going to have to bring him back to the task he wants to avoid no matter how mad he gets or what kind of tantrum he throws. Tantrums are not a solution. Developing the discipline it takes to do things you would rather not is far more important than having a perfectly behaved kid.

Compassion: I think I was too busy honoring Brendan for him to ever honor himself. I know that when you honor who you are as an individual, you tend to honor others for who they are. In some ways, I think this is about acceptance—acceptance of self and others. This means the wonderful parts of who we are, as well as the areas that require work. I think I need to start showing Brendan what that looks like by honoring my own boundaries, preferences, and so on, and that includes my desire for a home that we can all enjoy. This opens up so many new avenues for me to pursue as a mother.

Two weeks later: I wrote down, "What do I do to model for my son that I honor and accept myself?" This was a wake-up call. As it turns out, I don't. My focus has shifted from finding a strategy to get Brendan to pick up his toys (controlling others) to how I honor my desire for a reasonably organized home, and that means we all pick up our junk at least once a day. Amazing things happen when you start to model the character traits you hope your kids will embody. It's a work in progress, but one I am enjoying so much more than muscling my toddler into picking up his toys.

Step Six: Creating an Intentional Plan

Describe the routine, structure, or plan you want to implement.

- Clean out the toys by process of elimination. Toys left out repeatedly go into the "giveaway" bin and will be distributed once a month to our local charity.

- No more than three toys or activities are left out at any given time. Instead of talking, I calmly walk Brendan back to the toys and say, "As soon as you pick these toys up, you can take the toaster apart." If he refuses to pick the toys up, I pick them up and put them away for the day.

- Deal with meltdowns and tantrums in order to teach my son the more important trait, self-discipline.

Insights: First of all, the language that I use with my son has changed and therefore my attitude has changed. I used to start getting anxious at the first sound of a bin of blocks being dumped out, and now I know that one way or another they will get cleaned up. If they don't, ultimately it doesn't really matter. What matters is that our relationship does not revolve around a power struggle anymore. I explained to Brendan that in order to enjoy the privilege of having access to all his toys, he is required to pick them up when he is done playing with them.

If he chooses not to pick them up, I am at choice as to what I will do with them. I could pick them up and put them away. I may choose to put a toy in an undisclosed location if it is left out repeatedly, because a toy left out over and over again tells me that it isn't a very important toy.

He has responded really well to this and it seems to make sense to him. For the most part, he is willing to pick up after himself. What has changed the most though, is the energy that I was giving the whole situation. I didn't even realize the pressure that I was putting on my four-year-old to be completely neat and tidy and the power struggles that I was engaging in with my child.

Step Seven: Trusting Your Intuition

What do you know about your child that will ensure you have set up a structure that will work for him?

I know that my son responds well when he knows what is expected of him, and that means I can't just spring a new routine or a new rule on him. I know that the power struggles were his way of saying that he wants more control over his own stuff and that he wants and needs to feel more needed within the family. Giving him the freedom and opportunities to learn and master different tasks has helped him feel more capable, and this is showing up in other areas of his life.

Teens

Mike is dad to twin boys, Brett and William, age seventeen. He has coached his sons' teams for years and has always encouraged them to participate in multiple sports. Lately, when he comes home from work in the evening, he trips over something left in the mudroom. Mike says:

Last night it was a bag from swim team full of wet bathing suits and towels. It's always something, right inside the door. During hockey season, you have to climb over their stuff to get into the house. They need to know that there are other people living in this house and the mudroom isn't their personal sports' locker. They are just being lazy and inconsiderate and nothing that I say seems to get through to them. When they *do* put things away, it's not even in the right spot, they don't take care of equipment the way I was taught to, and they refuse to take my advice on how to store their things. I'm tired of their laziness and want them to learn the right way to care for their things."

Step One: Describing the Situation (in as few words as possible)

My seventeen-year-old sons leave their stuff in the mudroom, as if they own the space; after all these years of trying to get them to put their gear away, I have no idea what else to do. I'm done. **I give up.** Sometimes I just want them out of my house, so I don't have to deal with it anymore. They are lazy, selfish, and indulged boys. This tells me that the mistaken goal of behavior is **avoidance**, because I am at a loss as to what to do. I am feeling **hopeless and helpless.**

Step Two: Developing a Relationship Blueprint

Identify any negative labels you use with your children that influence their self-ideal.

At a loss for what to do, I feel as though my boys are just lazy, inconsiderate, spoiled, self-centered, ungrateful, and disrespectful and that I have to learn to live with it.

Replace the negative labels with positive attributes/qualities you want to use so your children develop a healthy self-ideal.

Hard working, considerate, grateful, respectful, and responsible. Big list for a dad who may or may not demonstrate all those attributes himself on any given day. The power in this exercise is in understanding that soon my kids will be grown men, and if they see themselves as lazy and inconsiderate as a result of my labels, it seems reasonable that they will continue to behave in these ways. I know there is so much more to them than my negative labels, but I have given myself permission to focus on their deficits, convincing myself that by doing so I was upholding my parental responsibilities. Vicki introduced me to her "don't feed the weed" idea, and that one visual made it possible for me to drop this idea and focus on the positives.

What parenting strategies do you use to manipulate your children into changing their behavior and what will you replace them with?

I demand, disconnect, and give up. It never occurred to me that the strategies I used to get my kids to do what I wanted them to do would be the same strategies they use to try to manipulate other people into doing what they want. Why doesn't anyone tell you this stuff when the kids are babies? I am a creature of habit and this is going to be hard for me, but I have my list of new strategies to try. I am committed to thinking of my boys as grown men with families of their own, and this is going to help me hold myself accountable. I believe that taking personal responsibility for your choices is a healthy strategy. Admitting when you are wrong, apologizing for your part in the misunderstanding, talking with an open mind, and a willingness to try what the other person is suggesting before ruling it out are also healthy strategies when dealing with other people in your personal or professional life. I have a lot to do to rebuild this relationship.

What qualities of a healthy relationship do you want to focus on that, over time, will influence or change this scenario in a positive way and support qualities found in a healthy relationship?

Respect, cooperation, and compassion are the qualities I most admire in the healthy relationships I have either been in or I have been fortunate enough to observe. And I understand that I have not been living the true meaning of those words. I have flushed out my convoluted ideas of respect and cooperation, and although it will be difficult to break old patterns, I know I can do this. The difficult one for me will be compassion. My own father was unrelenting and I equate compassion with weakness; yet, I am always drawn to individuals who feel comfortable and at ease showing compassion for themselves and others. I know that this trait will make a world of difference in my life with the boys now and for my boys as grown men who will someday be fathers.

Step Three: Fostering Independence

Have you been supporting their independence in this area?

I have spent so much time focusing on the boys and what I considered their deficits that I can honestly say that I have to completely rethink their level of competency in so many other areas of life.

How will you foster your children's independence in a way that will influence this situation and ensure they are independent and self-sufficient when they are adults?

As with the relationship blueprint exercise, I sat down with the boys and we made a list of all the areas of their lives where they are "rocking it," and I graciously accepted my place as the passenger in the backseat instead of the driver. I felt relieved, to tell you the truth. Then we made a list of the things they still wanted to learn before they left for college. Surprisingly, this list wasn't as long as I thought it would be. My boys have never been lazy. While I was busy finding what they did wrong, they had been working with other people to learn how to manage things like their finances and how to organize their schoolwork, sports schedules, social lives, and part-time jobs. In spite of me, they are remarkably prepared for life.

Step Four: Living with a Teen

What can you do in the moment that will move the action forward without making things worse?

When I trip over the stuff, I will walk away and keep things in perspective. It's stuff. It has nothing to do with respect or love or anything else. We can talk about the situation when we are all calm and I will express my expectations. They are young adults, not four-year-olds anymore. Who knows, if I give them a chance, they may have a better way to organize the mudroom so it is functional and easy to use.

Step Five: Raising an Adult

What character traits or life lessons can you teach in this situation that will benefit your children from age eighteen to eighty?

Once I updated my ideas about respect, it was easier for me to consider the character traits I wanted my boys to embody as adult men. I assure you, having men who can organize their sports gear was not on my list. What a blockhead I've been.

Self-respect: I can talk all day about how I want my boys to grow into men who have self-respect, but as they are growing into men, they are learning what respect looks like from me, and I have not been a very good role model. I want them to know their own value and worth and not live by other people's expectations or standards. I want them to walk away from people who make them feel badly about themselves or keep them from growing. I want them to have the dignity and strength to stand up for what they believe in. This all starts at home, within this family. I almost missed the boat, but I feel like I have some time to repair and really work on this. I know that my opinion matters to them, but I have to watch how I speak to the boys and what my motives are. And, I have to show respect for myself by setting limits, following through, and not acting like a teenage boy myself when I don't get my own way.

Flexibility: I see now that I cannot hope for my kids to grow up and become flexible adults if they are parented by an inflexible father. Flexibility will serve them well when they are grown men. In the workplace: the ability to switch gears, deal with the unexpected, and deal with different personalities. In their personal lives: finding a partner and finding a balance of needs and ways of doing things. As parents themselves: when they have kids of their own who aren't doing something exactly the way they want it done. My hope is that they will be flexible enough to adapt and bend and be open to other points of view. It is my responsibility to be flexible and model with my actions and reactions.

Humility: I want my kids to hold themselves in high regard and to have the confidence to go out into the world and succeed, and at the same time, I want them to accept others and their views and ways of doing things. This starts with me. More than anything I say, my children are watching what I do and who I am. This is my chance to be the person that I want my children to become.

Step Six: Creating an Intentional Plan

Describe the routine, structure, or plan you want to implement.

We sat down and had a very honest, open, and reasonable conversation. I admitted the mistakes that I had been making and let my boys know that I was committed to repairing the damage. We came to agreements around things left in the mudroom. My request was that their things were put away, in whatever way they saw fit as long as I didn't trip over them. Their request was that I keep my opinion on their organization to myself. Done.

Step Seven: Trusting Your Intuition

What do you know about your children that will ensure you have set up a structure that will work for them?

I know that Brett and William know how to put their equipment away and I was being completely unreasonable and unfair when communicating my expectations. I know that they distance themselves from me when they feel criticized, so I have to watch how they respond to me to gauge whether I am slipping back into old patterns. I also know that they have found ways to solve problems without my input, and although this is a hard pill to swallow, I am grateful that they knew where to go for support. I know that they deserve a father who has faith in their abilities and shows respect for the men they are becoming.

CHAPTER TEN

Sibling Squabbles

Sibling rivalry may be one of the most difficult dynamics for any parent to witness. It's heartbreaking to watch and listen as your kids tear each other apart and knowing what to do to change things can be confusing and frustrating. Here are two stories that illustrate the power the method has to bring a family closer together.

Toddlers

Maureen says:

I have three kids: four-year-old twins Anna and Amy and nine-year-old Molly. The fighting is bad. My twins bicker all day long about anything and everything. They grab, steal, yell, and tantrum multiple times a day. They have started hitting and biting each other and Molly. I'm really nervous that one of them could get seriously hurt. I feel like I need to be with them every second so that no one gets badly hurt. When I leave the room for even a few minutes, it's not long before I hear, "Moooooommmm, she stole my toy" or an "Aaaaaahhhhh, she's bugging me!" or a scream so loud that I can't imagine what the neighbors must think. They won't share and they rarely play together without incident. My oldest daughter, Molly, is a peacemaker and is always trying to play with her younger sisters and help things go smoothly. Thank goodness I have her or I don't know what I would do. I just want my girls to get along and be best friends, but with the younger two so challenging I am starting to feel like I've done something wrong as a mom to cause them to have such a horrible relationship with each other and with the rest of the family.

Step One: Describing the Situation (in as few words as possible)

This is the result of the four questions you ask yourself to determine the mistaken goal of behavior.

My four-year-old twins spend their time together yelling and screaming, and it is to the point where I can't leave the room for five minutes without needing to return to break up a fight or argument. I am **frustrated** during the day and exhausted at night. I have tried everything I can think of to bring peace to the house. This tells me that the mistaken goal of their behavior is **attention**.

Step Two: Developing a Relationship Blueprint

Identify any negative labels you use with your children that influence their self-ideal.

That's easy. I refer to them as selfish, demanding, unruly, and tyrannical; yes, I call my four-year-old twins tyrants.

Replace the negative labels with positive attributes/qualities you want to use so your children develop a healthy self-ideal.

I would like the girls to describe themselves as kind, considerate, loving, forgiving, and flexible. I understand now that I have to use those words, along with many others, in order for them to identify with them and see themselves in these ways. The challenge, of course, is in finding the moments when they actually demonstrate them even a little so I can, as Vicki says, anchor the words with the action, encouraging them to continue to cultivate those qualities for themselves. It's so easy when I am talking to other mothers to start complaining about the girls and I know this influences my next interaction with them. I can only imagine what will happen for me when I start using positive words to describe them. I imagine it will be so much easier for me to remain patient, compassionate, understanding, and firm with them when I am feeding my own mind these wonderful words.

What parenting strategies do you use to manipulate your children into changing their behavior and what will you replace them with?

I bribe, try to solve the problem for them, and separate them, but I haven't started teaching them how to cooperate, to solve problems together, to take a break from each other when they hit critical mass, or to deal with their frustration in constructive ways. Obviously, these skills take much longer to teach our kids, but they have to be taught if the girls are going to have the skills to navigate more complex relationships when they get older.

What qualities of a healthy relationship do you want to focus on that, over time, will influence or change this scenario in a positive way and support qualities found in a healthy relationship?

Self-Discipline and flexibility are the two qualities that come to mind that I misrepresent. I know I don't model self-discipline or self-control on many occasions, and I know I use those words with the girls when their behavior begins to escalate. I'll have to be sure and acknowledge when any of us are showing even the slightest bit of self-discipline in order for all of us to develop this quality. I also realize that I ask the girls to be flexible with me, but I am rarely flexible with them and this leads to power struggles so I can see both the immediate and long-term benefit of modeling a more flexible attitude.

Step Three: Fostering Independence

Have you been supporting their independence in this area?

No. I interfere. This rests on my shoulders. From birth, Anna and Amy have been "the twins" and "Molly's baby sisters." I haven't allowed them to own their own independence or individual place in this family.

How will you foster your children's independence in a way that will influence this situation and ensure they are independent and self-sufficient when they are adults?

- First, I will use the Timeline for Training to establish guidelines for teaching the younger girls how to take care of themselves and how to make a contribution to the family on a regular basis.

- I will support Molly's need to become socially mature and stop using her as the go-to babysitter.
- I will work with Molly to help establish family policies that concern all of us so that she feels she is being honored for who she is in the family.
- Give Amy and Anna more choices throughout the day and then hold them accountable for those choices.

Step Four: Living with Toddlers

What could you have done in the moment that would move the action forward without making things worse?

- Give myself permission to stay out of fights unless someone is in danger of getting seriously hurt.
- Ignore the yelling that is coming from the playroom.
- Lead the tattler to the Problem Board. (The Problem Board is an element of family meeting and provides a place for children to write their complaints using the "no name, no blame" format. During family meeting time is allotted each week to address a problem and come up with a solution. For more information about family meeting and the Problem Board please visit www.vickihoefle.com/family-meeting-30Gurus). Stop comparing my children and focus on their individual strengths.

Step Five: Raising Adults

What character traits or life lessons can you teach in this situation that will benefit your children from age eighteen to eighty?

The two traits that come to mind are individuality and cooperation. At first, I thought it didn't make sense to pair those two qualities, but when I really think about it, it makes perfect sense for my family.

Individuality: In a family of three girls that includes a set of twins, individuality is hard to come by. I will foster their sense of individuality by appreciating what makes them each unique and supporting their personal preferences. This will allow each to grow into an adult who understands the value of being her own person.

Cooperation: On the other hand, even a person with a great sense of individuality (autonomy) benefits from understanding the importance and necessity of cooperation. With family meetings, our family is connecting as a team and learning how to discuss and solve problems and cooperate as a group. I see how the skills they learn in family meeting will benefit them outside our home and in other relationships. This is a huge life lesson, and one that my girls will benefit from in adulthood.

Step Six: Creating an Intentional Plan

Describe the routine, structure, or plan you want to implement.

Family meetings: When Vicki first talked about family meetings, it didn't sound that powerful to me. However, once we committed to having a meeting every week, our family dynamic drastically improved.

- **Appreciations**: This has been such a gift, and something that I realize now I was not giving to my girls. I had no mental space to even think about what I appreciated about them, because of all the fighting. Now we all know, at least once a week, we will hear from each other what we notice and genuinely appreciate. We started an Appreciation Board; each day we put up a clean piece of paper, and throughout the day we stop to write down the things we appreciate about each other. This is helpful as we develop the habit of noticing and remembering. An added benefit is that, whenever there is even the slightest hint of an argument or someone is feeling down or discouraged, we walk them over and read out loud all the things their family appreciates about them. Everyone spends their time looking for things to appreciate about each other instead of nitpicking or squabbling.
- **Problem Board**: This was another game changer. My little tattlers have no more audience, when my response is, "That sounds like a problem for you. Go ahead and write it on the Problem Board and we'll discuss it at family meeting." Since Anna and Amy can't write yet, we borrowed Vicki's idea and put a pile of magazines, some safety scissors, and a glue stick in a basket, and now the girls are encouraged to find a picture of the problem, cut it out, and stick it on the board. Not only does this process keep me out of the problem in that moment, but the process of problem solving during family meeting is an amazing thing to watch my girls begin to learn.

Connections: Now that our entire relationship has shifted away from fighting and breaking up sibling squabbles, I have the time and space for making intentional connections with each of my kids individually. I set aside special time for each one of them and am working on developing relationships individually, as well as with all of us as a unit.

Step Seven: Trusting Your Intuition

What do you know about your daughters that will ensure you have set up a structure that will work for them?

Comparing my girls and labeling each of them inadvertently created a situation in which my youngest daughters thought that they had to fight, yell, and scream at each other in order to get my attention and define their place in the family, while my oldest daughter came to believe that she needed to be perfect all the time. Now that I have started to figure this out, I can say with confidence that I am learning so much more about each of my daughters. This will allow their independence, confidence, and our relationship to flourish. Conflict is uncomfortable for Molly, so using family meetings will help her learn to deal with conflict in constructive ways. She genuinely loves spending time with younger children, so I will find opportunities outside of the house for her to work with kids.

Teens

My teenagers are in that "hate your sibling" phase, and I need to figure out how to get them out of it. My sixteen-year-old daughter, Mackenna, and my fourteen-year- old son, Matthew, cannot be in the same room without a fight of some sort. Mackenna is moody and often treats her younger brother like a pest. She is so nasty to him that most of the time I end up stepping in so I can stick up for him, and then I get in to a screaming match of my own with her. Matthew can be just as difficult. He bugs her with digs about a new pimple or taunts about a boy she likes. He tattles on her, which drives me crazy, but I feel like I have to listen to him because she gets so out of control. I swear one of these days she might go over the edge. I am drawn into their drama all the time. They are too old to be tattling on each other, but they do. I am disappointed in both of them.

Step One: Describing the Situation (in as few words as possible)

This is the result of the four questions you ask yourself to determine the mistaken goal of behavior.

My kids don't get along well and there is constant drama in my house. Mackenna lashes out at her brother and is nasty and disrespectful when anyone disagrees with her. My **heart breaks** when she behaves this way because she has never been treated in this matter. Matthew is fourteen years old but still tattles like he did when he was five. While I find that **annoying**, I also feel badly that he has to deal with his nasty older sister. I get involved in their fights, I lecture, I punish, and then I just scream at them to knock it off. This tells me that the mistaken goal of behavior for Matty is **attention** and for Mackenna it is **revenge.**

Step Two: Developing a Relationship Blueprint

Identify any negative labels you use with your children that influence their self-ideal.

When I am at my worst, I refer to my kids as moody, oversensitive, nasty, insensitive, bullying tattle-tales.

Replace the negative labels with positive attributes/qualities you want to use so your children develop a healthy self-ideal.

I know my kids bring more to the table than their negative labels, but truthfully, it was hard for me to nail down positive qualities and attributes that I could start focusing on. After a bit of reflection I came up with several that I almost never acknowledge: kind, considerate, resourceful, hardworking, and focused. I can already see that MacKenna is starting to identify with the negative words I use when I am angry with her. I know she must be thinking, "Well, if that's what you think of me, I won't disappoint you." It's a cycle that I never even considered. I can see that Matthew is starting to think of himself as a victim instead of a strong, intelligent, competent problem solver. Butting in and getting angry at them isn't doing anything for them or me. It's time to stop.

What parenting strategies do you use to manipulate your children into changing their behavior and what will you replace them with?

I use disappointment to shame my daughter and then I punish her by taking away privileges. I save my son, which sends the message to him that he is weak and can't take care of himself. Both of these strategies would make for a disastrous adult relationship. Vicki talks about teaching kids how to get along instead of focusing on trying to stop the fighting, and I can see that I could use those strategies in many of the challenges we face. The kids are close and they love each other, but I haven't provided them with an environment where they can nurture that relationship and learn to support each other.

What qualities of a healthy relationship do you want to focus on that, over time, will influence or change this scenario in a positive way and support qualities found in a healthy relationship?

Collaboration and acceptance of self and others are my biggies. I'll be honest and admit that I do not collaborate very well with the kids. I know I am indulging myself and being a lousy role model to the kids. I have to look at these two as young adults and treat them like I do my coworkers, and we will be on our way to redefining this powerful word. Acceptance of self and others means, at least for me, that you can look yourself in the mirror and accept the good with the bad, the strengths with the weakness, and work on the areas that need refining. And when you can look at yourself with acceptance, you can accept others for who and what they are. That is a gift in any relationship and it starts by accepting that I mess up and accepting that my kids are amazing and that they mess up. I can already sense the shift in me and the lifting of the pressure I put on myself.

Step Three: Fostering Independence

Have you been supporting your children's independence in this area?

No. I thought of independence as something that I could give to my kids. For example, I let Mackenna borrow my car now that she has her license, thinking I was giving her independence by letting her go to the store alone. I let Matthew walk to the football game the other night with his buddies after dark because I wanted him to feel independent. Boy, am I off base. I can't give them independence. Independence is not about *letting* them do things. Independence is about fostering the skill set and experience within our family, and then allowing them to move beyond our threshold and continue to practice.

How will you foster your children's independence in a way that will influence this situation and ensure they are independent and self-sufficient when they are adults?

- Balance privileges and responsibilities: a fair and equitable system needs to be available to everyone based on their abilities and maturity level. This process makes it so much easier to support each of them as individuals and see them as high-functioning, intelligent, thoughtful kids.
- Support decision making: extend an invitation to both of the children to participate in family policy. My role is to hold them accountable to the decisions and policies we put in place, and this includes how we will handle their attitudes and actions toward each other.
- Help them prepare for departure: spend time with each of them separately talking with them about what is ahead for them, so that they get the sense that this is their time to take on more of their life without our constant input.

Step Four: Living with Teens

What can you do in the moment that will move the action forward without making things worse?

- Stay out of it!
- Walk away
- Institute the Problem Board, so we can settle it later.

Step Five: Raising an Adult

What character traits or life lessons can you teach in this situation that will benefit your child from age eighteen to eighty?

Understanding: I want Mackenna and Matthew to become adults who are understanding and compassionate about other people's feelings, their situations, and their struggles. My hope is that when Mackenna and Matthew have little spats, they will have the tools and the understanding to get through them, forgive each other, and move on. When that happens, they will be on their way toward becoming understanding and compassionate adults. This trait does not appear overnight and my role is to create an environment where they can practice this skill with support from me, not interference.

Openness: Being open with those you are close to means talking about your weaknesses, your fears, your worries, and your dreams. When you feel safe enough and comfortable enough to open up to another person, you have created something special and lasting. In order for my kids to develop this quality, I am going to have to show them what it looks like by being open with them. This will be a change for me, as I shut down so many of their conversations because my energy is zapped by the nastiness. When they need to talk to me, to open up about their lives, I am resentful and I often say something snarky or dismissive. If I want my children to develop a healthy quality that will serve them well as adults, I must change my behavior first.

Step Six: Creating an Intentional Plan

Describe the routine, structure, or plan you want to implement.

At first, I was completely overwhelmed trying to figure out where to start. When I discovered that the kids had different mistaken goals of behavior and I had such different things to work on in each of our relationships, I felt lost. Slowly, though, it has started to make sense. The issue of the kids fighting needed to be addressed, but before that could happen I needed to make shifts in my own behavior and reactions. Next, we put some of Vicki's suggestions into place.

Family meeting: This is my favorite. Here we talk about family news and problems and we give appreciations. My kids are giving each other appreciations. This is huge for us. And my appreciations to the kids happen all week long. It never dawned on me before to verbalize what I appreciated in the moment, however, I now understand that showing appreciation is supporting all of the qualities I think are imperative in a healthy relationship and also the character traits I think are necessary for a successful adult life. Beyond that, letting Mackenna know that she has taught me something or letting Matthew know that I enjoy spending time with him is healing for all of us. Family meetings also allow my kids an opportunity to voice their opinions in the family and see that we want to work together with them. Introducing the Problem Board has made tattling pointless, because I just point them toward the board and let them know we'll talk about it in a meeting.

Timeline for Training: For Matthew, this has really been a big one. That kid was so eager to learn and take ownership of his life. I can't believe I didn't see this—well, yes, I can believe it, because he has been trying to tell me for years that he was ready for more and I just refused to listen to the clues he was throwing my way. I am no longer hovering or fixing his mistakes or saving him. I'm trusting in the training process and I'm trusting that my son will be just fine.

No more interfering: I don't get involved in the kids' arguments anymore. I don't come running if Mathew does call. I don't yell and threaten Mackenna. I just stay out of it. This is so freeing and I feel so much less stressed if I do hear them bickering. Because I am no longer getting involved, the fights lose steam quickly and the kids move on to other things.

Agreements: We're still working on how to use agreements, but for now the kids each identified the one thing that really bothers them, and that they feel is interfering with their relationship. They have agreed to make an effort to stop doing that one thing (listed below) to develop this new approach. Just listening to them discuss their feelings and their willingness to make an effort was such a step in the right direction.

- Matthew agrees not to interrupt or tease Mackenna while she's on the phone or with friends.
- Mackenna agrees to refrain from calling Matthew names.

Step Seven: Trusting Your Intuition

What do you know about your son and daughter that will ensure you have set up a structure that will work for them?

Mackenna is the oldest and she often feels that her position in the family is being threatened by her younger brother. She has a tendency to blame and feel as though I am picking sides, and she is right, I *was* picking sides. I have to understand that when she blames, she is feeling threatened, and I need to show my compassion and understanding for her feelings. My job will be to connect with her and communicate to her in every way possible that no matter what happens, she counts, she matters, and if there were a hundred kids or a a thousand kids or a hundred thousand kids at the mall, I would choose to be her mom every damn time.

Matthew is high energy with a huge desire to be active. He gets bored easily and likes to mix it up a bit for fun. I will offer him choices, teach him as many life skills as I can, let him practice at every opportunity, ask him questions, and do whatever it takes to tire him out. Vicki reminds us that tired kids don't have the energy to make mischief. My job will be to keep Matthew so engaged in productive tasks that he drops at the end of every day.

CHAPTER ELEVEN

Snark, Sass, and "Whatevs"

No one wants to raise kids who are rude, disrespectful, or dismissive and yet, more and more kids are throwing the sass around with no filtering or editing or notion that it is just plain unacceptable. It's possible to turn the tide and bring back your easy-to-be-with kids who show themselves and others the respect we all deserve.

School-Aged

Leslie and Jared are the parents of three children: six-year-old Jeffrey, eight-year-old Nicholas, and eleven-year-old Erin. They shared the following with me:

Erin started copping an attitude with us a few years ago. We didn't pay much attention to it at first because we were busy with three kids, full-time careers, and maintaining a marriage. Over the last few years the attitudes have become unbearable. Not only is Erin's attitude bad, her siblings have decided to mimic her, and now all three of them talk to us like we are second-class citizens who work for them. They roll their eyes at us, say things like "whatever," walk away from us when we are talking to them, and tell us they don't have to listen to us. It is embarrassing, humiliating, and disturbing, and neither of us knows what to do. We have tried lectures and punishments. We ignore them and talk to them rationally. We have tried making agreements with them but nothing, and I mean nothing, is working. We are befuddled and looking for anything that might turn things around.

Step One: Describing the Situation (in as few words as possible)

This is the result of the four questions you ask yourself to determine the mistaken goal of behavior.

Our three children are disrespectful and throw the sass our way every chance they get. We are **hurt** and we do not know what to do to turn things around. This tells us that the mistaken behavior is **revenge**.

> **Note from Vicki:** Leslie and Jared understand that each of the children may have individual mistaken goals of behavior, but things are so bad that they are working from the perspective that all of the kids are feeling hurt and thus are trying to hurt their parents. This could change as the two make changes to their parenting and learn more about the kids.

Step Two: Developing a Relationship Blueprint

Identify any negative labels you use with your children that influence their self-ideal.

We are so discouraged as parents. We have a difficult time thinking about our kids as anything other than snarky, sassy, rude, disrespectful, and mean.

Replace the negative labels with positive attributes/qualities you want to use so your children develop a healthy self-ideal.

Kind, cooperative, flexible, resilient, courageous, responsible, and supportive to name a few. This is how we want our kids to see themselves, but it is so dang hard to remember, let alone foster these attributes and qualities when they are so nasty to us. This is the crux of the problem. We decided at some point that we wouldn't say anything positive about the kids until they stopped acting like brats. That just made things worse. We are taking a leap of faith and we are going to start acknowledging any positive qualities we notice no matter how the kids are acting. Logically it makes sense that their behavior will improve, because the way we treat them and talk about them is improving, but it can be a hard pill to swallow if you don't see the bigger picture.

What parenting strategies do you use to manipulate your children into changing their behavior and what will you replace them with?

We throw the sass right back at them and then punish them by taking away something they care about, like the computer, a special show they like to watch, or coming with us on our nightly walk. We live in a cycle of who can hurt whom the most. We also give up, which I think sends the message to the kids that we don't care. The new strategies are going to require a lot of practice on our part. We take their sass so personally right now that it's hard to imagine staying respectful in how we deal with it. We decided that we could leverage our own experience in the professional world to attack this problem. If we modify some of the strategies we use with our coworkers we can imagine changing the climate of our home in a matter of a few weeks.

What qualities of a healthy relationship do you want to focus on that, over time, will influence or change this scenario in a positive way and support qualities found in a healthy relationship?

Respectful and open communication: We both took classes in nonviolent communication and we pride ourselves on being open and honest with our communication. We know that it takes practice and that you have to establish guidelines when talking about difficult or emotionally charged subjects. We listen with empathy and take into consideration the other person's point of view. We can table a conversation when we see that the conversation has become personal and there is a chance that it will deteriorate.

Going through this exercise was essential. After all the back patting, we realize that we do not practice these qualities with our kids. In fact, if we summarize our approach to raising our kids, it's the role of "superior teacher." We talk at the children, not with them; we make the rules for the children because we think we know best; we listen to the kids but have no intention of using any of their suggestions or solutions, so we are patronizing. What we have done is drilled into them how they should speak to us and treat us. We want them to be compatible with our lives, we want them to share our values, and have never considered what their values might be or what they mean to them.

We want our kids to answer any question we ask them with full disclosure (because, you know, we are such awesome, open communicators) but we never modeled these qualities to our children. Shame on us for acting surprised when they treat us with a mild form of contempt. They are communicating clearly that things need to change. I am ashamed that we actually thought this was their doing.

Step Three: Fostering Independence

Have you been supporting their independence in this area?

Certainly not. We would have said yes before we finished the exercise above, but that would have been another pat on the back about how fabulous we are at teaching our kids to be socially responsible people by turning off the lights and recycling. This further explains their contemptuous attitude toward us. We treat them like morons instead of like the insightful, intelligent, resourceful kids they are. All of their behavior is in response to how we have been treating them.

How will you foster your children's independence in a way that will influence this situation and ensure they are independent and self-sufficient when they are adults?

• Use the Timeline for Training: we have so much work to do, but with this nifty tool, we can tackle the self, home, and, to a certain extent, social skills in an organized way that won't overwhelm the kids. This tool allows us to support them emotionally, and to show them we trust them and have faith in their abilities. We are hopeful that they will start to forgive us for being so self-righteous.

• Offer choices: give them as many as we possibly can during the day and then whenever possible support those choices. As Vicki says, "If it isn't morally or physically dangerous, go for it."

• Ask questions: discover what they are thinking instead of telling them what to think. Open up conversations that are about nothing more than listening to how they process information, what's important to them, what frustrates them, and how they work through their problems.

- Invite them to help form family policy: ask them to play a more active role in policies for the family without putting our two cents in about "what we have learned over the years and why they should just follow our lead." We have already mastered this skill. Our job is to let our children become experts.

Step Four: Living with School-Aged Children

What can you do in the moment that will move the action forward without making things worse?

- No matter what the kids throw our way, we could actually try living our core values and treat them with respect and love, remove ourselves from the situation, and stop taking it so personally. This is our time to be the people we want our children to become. This is the time for us to demonstrate how you treat people you love. Over time, I am confident that we will all remember that we love each other and will start treating each other with the dignity and respect we all deserve.
- Walk in our children's shoes. Take time to remember our children are developing their views on the world. Meet them where they are, remove the emotion, and focus on understanding their perspective.

Step Five: Raising an Adult

What character traits or life lessons can you teach in this situation that would benefit your child from age eighteen to eighty?

Understanding, acceptance, and empathy: We have been so focused on doing things our way and being the experts in our children's lives that we have squashed our children's sense of belonging. Our children need to understand that they matter—regardless of their viewpoint or behavior. By modeling and living our values, and by sending the message that our children always have a place here and we are their biggest champions, we are confident that we will see a shift in their behavior over time.

Step Six: Creating an Intentional Plan

Describe the routine, structure, or plan you want to implement.

The plan is simple: until we repair the relationship with the kids, we are not putting any consequences or systems or plans in place. We will build the relationship and then, if the sass continues, we can come up with a family policy that addresses it in a respectful way.

We did, however, work as a family to create a more unified morning routine and, lo and behold, that exercise exposed more of our "superior thinking tricks." In the end, we asked the kids to create one that they thought would work for all of us and we committed to trying it for an entire week and then evaluating its success. As of today, we are still using the routine they created for the family, and because it came from them, they are making small adjustments to take into consideration the unique ways we all move through the morning. It's fascinating and inspiring.

Step Seven: Trusting Your Intuition

What do you know about your children that will ensure you have set up a structure that will work for them?

We have three kids with three very different points of view, preferences, temperaments, and styles of moving through the world.

Erin is quiet and introspective. She needs time to process information, to turn things over and over to be sure it makes sense to her, and only then can she make a decision she feels comfortable with. When we talk at her, give her direction, and treat her like she is three years old instead of a capable preteen, she shuts down and, we can admit now, the snarky attitude is what she does to get back at us. We misunderstood her quietness as a sign of contentment and were congratulating ourselves on raising such a self-contained daughter.

Nicholas is in many ways a very typical middle child in that he sees himself as the peacekeeper. Strong negative emotions or conflict are really upsetting for him, as is the instability in our daily planning, and oftentimes my wife and I change plans midstream when we are "inspired" to go off on an adventure. We can see now that by doing this we throw Nicholas into uncharted territory, and his anxiety goes up and his behavior deteriorates. We have to be more sensitive to his desire for harmony, and that means including him more, being consistent, and teaching him how to engage in healthy conflict where everyone is emotionally safe.

Jeffrey is both charismatic and energetic. I think we have overlooked his need to be taken seriously as a family member who has ideas and solutions and thoughts he wants to share. We often disregard what he says because he is our youngest. How insulting to him. Jeffrey learns by doing, not by someone talking to him about what he should or should not do, so allowing him to experience natural consequence and then supporting him when he melts down is going to send a strong message that we believe in him and know that he can handle whatever life throws his way.

Teens

Jeff is dad to sixteen-year-old Devin and is struggling to understand his son:

I have always looked forward to getting home from work and sitting down with my family after a long day. We are all going in many directions these days, so it's a treat when everyone is home for dinner and willing to sit down and visit. Lately, though, my son is giving my wife and me serious attitude. He walks around with a chip on his shoulder, rolls his eyes, and always seems utterly annoyed by us. A lot of the time it seems like he's living on a different planet. He doesn't seem to care about much of anything these days. It doesn't matter what we say about respect, what threats we make about grounding him or making him miss football practice, or what lectures we give him about being more pleasant with the family and more willing to help out and spend time with us—nothing changes. He seems ticked off from the moment he wakes up, and rarely do we spend five minutes with him before he's rude to one of us or just staring off into space blankly, completely ignoring the rest of the family. I don't know how to reach him or get through to him, and at this point I'm just sick of trying. How is he ever going to make it through a college interview or land a job if he walks around with such a bad attitude? I've been at such a loss with Devin that I recently told him he's being a punk and if he doesn't stop with the attitude and rudeness that I'm done trying with him.

Step One: Describing the Situation (in as few words as possible)

This is the result of the four questions you ask yourself to determine the mistaken goal of behavior.

I am feeling **helpless** over the state of my relationship with my son, Devin, and I am starting to give up on ever having a decent relationship with him. He has a crummy attitude and is completely miserable whenever he's around the family. All of this lets me know that his mistaken goal of behavior is **avoidance.**

Step Two: Developing a Relationship Blueprint

Identify any negative labels you use with your children that influence their self-ideal.

This is difficult because I feel at such a loss, but I really believe my child is unplugged, disengaged, and self-absorbed.

Replace the negative labels with positive attributes/qualities you want to use so your children develop a healthy self-ideal.

Self-respect, drive, personal responsibility, flexible in nature, and honest. I have imagined my son as a grown man, and the image I have right now isn't good. I see a man I might be ashamed to call my son and I am ashamed of myself for feeling this way. Because of the way I feel, I have to start slow and work with only one or two attributes I know my son has but doesn't demonstrate right now, and those would be that he is a very articulate and effective communicator and he is very introspective. In spite of the turmoil in the house, these qualities continue to shine through, I just haven't capitalized on them.

What parenting strategies do you use to manipulate your children into changing their behavior and what will you replace them with?

I yell, belittle, shame, threaten, and let him know I disapprove of his behavior. Obviously, these are not strategies that will work in healthy adult relationships, but it's what I use with my son. The strategy that makes the most sense to me right now is to start inviting Devin to share his thoughts on family decisions and ask him to help me solve a problem I might be having with a coworker or customer. Because he is so reflective in his thinking, this could draw him out and give us some common ground to build on. I also need to manage my own feelings and emotions and act like a grown man. I was his age once and I know how challenging life can be. It doesn't help that there is all this stress at home and that Devin may be feeling like I abandoned him when he needs me most to be on his side.

What qualities of a healthy relationship do you want to focus on that, over time, will influence or change this scenario in a positive way and support qualities found in a healthy relationship?

Responsibility: Like so many other parents I know, I throw the word responsibility around without considering how I am modeling this attribute for my kids. Not only do I want my son to learn to be a responsible adult, I want him to be responsible for his role in the relationships he creates. As with everything, this starts with me holding myself responsible for my behavior and my actions. I have been hiding behind responsibility as it applies to my career, focusing on controlling a situation to prevent a negative outcome. I see clearly that part of being a responsible human being is the ability to deal effectively with any situation. My job is to help Devin develop the skills to take responsibility for his contribution in the deterioration of our relationship and to bounce back and move forward when situations that he can't control have negative outcomes.

Honesty: My wife and I have drilled into our kids that you have to be honest with yourself in order to be honest with others. Okay, I could go on for a long time here about how I haven't been honest with myself, and what a mess that has caused, but I'll refrain. Suffice it to say that this is another area where we will work with the kids to define the word honesty and how it applies to the family in general and to each of us individually.

Step Three: Fostering Independence

Have you been supporting his independence in this area?

No. I have been pushing him, directing him, and overpowering him, but not fostering his own sense of independence and self-reliance.

How will you foster your child's independence in a way that will influence this situation and ensure he is independent and self-sufficient when he is an adult?

- Include Devin and give him an important role in helping redefine family policies, guidelines, and rules. This, more than anything, will influence the kind of future leader he will be, and that will serve him in every area of his life.

• Use the Timeline for Training to figure out where Devin is in the bigger scheme of things, and then sit down and ask him what he wants to tackle first and how he wants to tackle it.

• Trust him to make decisions and then allow him a chance to experience the successes and failures without swiping the success out from underneath him or gloating when he messes up.

• Ask. Don't tell.

• Realize the importance of fostering resilience and courage in my son so that Devin is prepared for life's challenges, instead of trying to prevent them.

Step Four: Living with a Teen

What can you do in the moment that will move the action forward without making things worse?

Well, truthfully, if I put the work into this relationship the way I now understand that I need to, Devin might not walk around so ticked off and distant all the time. So in a moment when he gives me an attitude, I might ask him, "What's up, you seem off?" Or say, "Everything okay?" Or, "Is there anything I can do to help?" I will let him know that I am right here and willing to support him. It is imperative that I stop taking his behavior personally so I can stay positive and loving no matter what attitude he displays.

Step Five: Raising an Adult

What character traits or life lessons can you teach in this situation that will benefit your child from age eighteen to eighty?

Resilience: I wish I had been more resilient after losing my job. Maybe then we wouldn't be in this spot. I let it ruin me for a while and it completely changed my view of my kids' futures. I didn't know how to bounce back or how to find the resources I needed to help put things in perspective. My pride was destroyed and along with it my ability to rebound and rebuild. No matter what happens in life, I know my kids are going to need a reserve of resilience if they are going to be able to power through and come out on the other side. So how do I support that in my own kids? Easy: allow them plenty of opportunities to experience disappointment, embarrassment, failure, rejection, and betrayal and be there to support them but allow them to move through the experience on their own.

Courage: I want my kids to have the courage to go for their dreams and not worry about playing it safe, to love without limits and risk the heartache. I want them to find the courage to say yes and to say no, to say I'm sorry and to admit when they are wrong, to hold other people accountable for their actions and to forgive easily and often.

Confidence: I was really confident in my job skills and in how important I was to the company, but I had no confidence when it came to dealing with adversity or taking a reasonable risk toward a new career, or confidence that I could support my family without my long-standing job. I didn't have confidence in my ability to be honest about how hurt and scared I was when I lost my job, and I didn't have the confidence to ask for help. I can't build my son's confidence up for him, but I can certainly stop tearing it down. I will absolutely change my ways and begin to show faith in him, and with that I hope comes a renewed sense of confidence for him.

Step Six: Creating an Intentional Plan

Describe the routine, structure, or plan you want to implement.

I have not really set up a structure but rather restructured my own way of viewing Devin and my role as his father. I have hope that this shift will benefit him now and in the long run. I didn't even realize how amazing my kid was until I went through these exercises with Vicki and took some accountability for my part in the breakdown of our relationship. After I apologized to him for my mistakes and let him know how committed I am going forward, his moods around the house began to shift. He is more willing to have a conversation and to answer questions that his mom and I ask. He even joined me for breakfast out at the local bakery the other day. I am making an effort to connect with him around the things that he is interested in and passionate about without expressing any pressure or judgment.

I have to be honest; it's hard to change my ways. This is real work. I want what is best for my kid and I still hope very much that he has a successful future and never has to deal with a job loss like I did. But now I realize that in order for him to be strong, confident, and resilient in his adult life, he needs a solid foundation, a place to practice and not be picked apart and judged. I am still a work in progress and I remind myself to find the faith that he will be fine in whatever career he chooses. In the meantime, I'm keeping that baggage to myself and not putting it on him. That alone has made a difference in our relationship and I am so grateful for that.

Step Seven: Trusting Your Intuition

What do you know about your son that will ensure you have set up a structure that will work for him?

I have missed really knowing who my son is, how he views the world around him, what energizes him, and what exhausts him. If I think back to when he was a child, I would say that he is curious and extremely compassionate. He wants to understand how things work and to understand other people and their views. I remember now that he asked really insightful questions when he was young, and my wife and I were struck with how interested he seemed to be in our answers when we explained things to him. But we talked with him then, not at him. So if I use what I know about my son from his childhood, I think I can be the father he needs and deserves and not the father who thinks he knows best. This is liberating and exciting.

CHAPTER TWELVE

Homework Hassles

Homework is responsible for an increase in power struggles, fractured relationships, and disconnection between parents and their kids, but it doesn't have to be this way. Two families share how the method allowed them to reframe the homework hassles and reclaim quality time with their kids.

School-Aged

Mark is a stay-at-home dad to his three kids. His older two children are in high school and have always done well in school. Simon, his ten-year-old, is another story altogether:

Education is very important to my wife and me. Not only do we expect the kids to maintain an A average in all of their studies, I tutor them after school in subjects that I know will give them a head start in college. My two older sons have never given us any trouble with their studies and put the extra time into their homework, but Simon does not seem to care at all about his education. Every day is a battle with him around homework, and some days it feels like I spend more time fighting with him than tutoring him in new subjects. We have taken all his sports and extracurricular activities away and now we have started to take away time with his friends. He can sit at his workstation for hours wasting time. I don't understand why he doesn't just get the work done so he can go about his life. I am really disappointed in my son and his lack of commitment to his education. I don't know what else I can do to get him to do his work.

Step One: Describing the Situation (in as few words as possible)

This is the result of the four questions you ask yourself to determine the mistaken goal of behavior.

My ten-year-old refuses to do his regular homework. He wastes his time, is disrespectful, and is not bothered when I take away his sports, hobbies, and social time. I am so **disappointed** that he doesn't appreciate everything his mother and I are trying to do to ensure he gets into a good college, so he can get a good job and make a good life for himself. This tells me his mistaken behavior is **revenge.**

Step Two: Developing a Relationship Blueprint

Identify any negative labels you use with your children that influence their self-ideal.

My son is stubborn, lazy, manipulative, and apathetic. I can't find any way to motivate him.

Replace the negative labels with positive attributes/qualities you want to use so your children develop a healthy self-ideal.

Confident in abilities, strong work ethic, and responsible. No where in this list of attributes I hope my son or any of my kids use to describe themselves has words like compassion, kindness, joy, or flexibility. I am so focused on performance, that I have completely overlooked the other side of what makes for amazing human beings. My own father was very intimidating and demanded excellence in everything I did. I was a very cold, emotionally distant young man and it took years of working with mentors and eventually a therapist for me to understand my true nature and allow other sides of my personality to emerge. Unfortunately, they have gone underground again and I am repeating the unhealthy cycle my father started.

What parenting strategies do you use to manipulate your children into changing their behavior and what will you replace them with?

I deny and withhold everything that Simon loves and brings him joy. We are setting a poor example for our son. I can't even consider being successful with other strategies until I flush out my goal for wanting Simon to do well in school, get into a good college, and to trust that I know what is best for him. I think at the crux of this challenge is me thinking I know what is best for my son and that implies that I don't think he knows what is best. If he enters adult life with this belief about himself and the idea that he can either force his will on others or that others can force their will on him, his life will feel like a constant battle. The most reasonable thing for me to do at this point is to take a less-is-more-approach and start stepping away from the entire homework/education issue.

What qualities of a healthy relationship do you want to focus on that, over time, will influence or change this scenario in a positive way and support how qualities found in a healthy relationship?

I misrepresent many of the words I use with all of my kids. I talk to them about how they should show respect, how they should model cooperation, how they should strive to be men of their word, how they should show compassion for other people when they struggle. And that's all well and good, but if they had to define those words by my actions, well, that would be interesting. I know what I have to do. I have to look all these words up, write down the definition and then I have to decide how I am going to model them each and every day until my kids learn their true meaning. Humbling experience to be sure.

Step Three: Fostering Independence

Have you been supporting his independence in this area?

No, not at all. I have been interrupting any chance he had of becoming more independent in this area.

How will you foster your child's independence in a way that will influence this situation and ensure he is independent and self-sufficient when he is an adult?

- Start listening to Simon when he tells me about how, where, and when he wants to do his homework.
- Take a break from all the extra tutoring and allow him to be a kid.

- Provide Simon with more privacy and autonomy.
- Use the Timeline for Training tool to investigate where Simon is in his development of self, home, social, and life skills.
- Create a plan to teach him how to do more for himself.
- I will adopt Vicki's language and use "Would you be willing to..." instead of "Do it now."

Step Four: Living with a School-Aged Child

What can you do in the moment that will move the action forward without making things worse?

- Refuse to fight with Simon. Nothing positive is ever accomplished once we both decide that the fight is on.
- Walk away and revisit the issue when we are both calm.
- Show respect for him and his preferences.
- Model a cooperative attitude by trying things his way.

Step Five: Raising an Adult

What character traits or life lessons can you teach in this situation that will benefit your child from age eighteen to eighty?

Self-knowledge: Simon isn't his older brothers and he is going to make his own path in life. When I treat him like an equal member of the family, one who is an individual with his own preferences and styles, and listen to him he will begin to understand himself and the way he moves through the world in a deeper way. I will ask Simon questions to activate his thinking. I can learn from his insight. The more he shares his thoughts out loud with others, the more confidence he will have in creating a life that has meaning for him.

Confidence: Confidence is born from experience. Experience is a balance of failures and successes, of trying solutions that work and ones that flop. Experiences build on trial and error and in taking risks to try a new way. Confidence builds on itself and gains momentum the more you depend on yourself to work through life's challenges. Simon must see that I have confidence in his abilities if he is ever going to have confidence in himself.

Step Six: Creating an Intentional Plan

Describe the routine, structure, or plan you want to implement.

- Decide with Simon when, where, and for how long he will work to complete his homework.
- Do not check his work. Allow the school to inform me if he begins to slide in any of his subjects.
- Allow Simon to decide which, if any, extra subjects he wants to study.

Step Seven: Trusting Your Intuition

What do you know about your child that will ensure you have set up a structure that will work for him?

Simon has a very different biorhythm than his older siblings. When he is high, he needs lots of physical activity to keep him in balance, and forcing him to study at certain times was interfering with his natural rhythm. When Simon is quiet, he is focused and calm and can retain what he is hearing or reading. If I follow his lead, I can capitalize on the calm moments to support him in his schoolwork. This also models cooperation, and it shows I support him and that I have faith in him. I know that he is used to taking a backseat to his older siblings and he gains attention by being disagreeable. When we include him in more decision-making opportunities, he will feel like an equal in the family.

Teens

Halley is mom to fifteen-year-old Quinn. She says:

Quinn puts off doing his homework until the morning it's due. I'm on him every afternoon when he gets home from practice, but I don't get anywhere with him. He won't show me his assignments and never does his work in the afternoon or in the evening. He ends up getting up in the morning and rushing through his work at six o'clock in the morning, when he should be downstairs eating breakfast with the rest of us. This affects the vibe at home and his grades at school are slipping. I am angry that he has been neglecting his schoolwork and I have tried everything to get through to him. I lecture, threaten to keep him home from soccer, and the other day I was so fired up that I ended up grounding him.

Step One: Describing the Situation (in as few words as possible)

This is the result of the four questions you ask yourself to determine the mistaken goal of behavior.

I feel like I have no control over my fifteen-year-old son, Quinn. He doesn't listen to anything I say. His attitude is bad and his grades are slipping. I feel **angry** about Quinn's nasty attitude and lack of willingness to cooperate. This tells me that his mistaken goal of behavior is **power**.

Step Two: Developing a Relationship Blueprint

Identify any negative labels you use with your children that influence their self-ideal.

When it comes to homework and family, my son is unmotivated, lazy, rude, and entitled.

Replace the negative labels with positive attributes/qualities you want to use so your children develop a healthy self-ideal.

Engaged, committed, team player/cooperative, enthusiastic, and reliable. I had to consider who my son was in other areas of his life and suddenly a host of positive attributes presented themselves. I have been overlooking all of them because I was so focused on what wasn't working. Isn't that what we are supposed to do as parents, focus on the areas that need work? Well, I focused so much of my attention there, that I forgot that I have an amazing son who is already well on his way to establishing the kinds of attributes and qualities that will make him a delight to be in relationship with

What parenting strategies do you use to manipulate your children into changing their behavior and what will you replace them with?

Threatening, lecturing, belittling, and comparing. I could go on, but I understand where this question is leading and I am excited at the possibilities. Here is my "aha." The only strategy that matters is the strategy that sends the message to my son that he is a great human being now and that I accept him for who he is now, and that I will do whatever I can to support the person he is and the person he is becoming. That is all I really want in my most intimate relationships and I believe it is the foundation for every healthy relationship I have ever been in. Everything else is a result of this one underlying belief.

What qualities of a healthy relationship do you want to focus on that, over time, will influence or change this scenario in a positive way and support qualities found in a healthy relationship?

Personal integrity: Everyone I respect has defined this idea in a very personal and unique way. When I was younger, I wrote up the attributes and traits that I wanted to embody and wrote a statement: I live with personal integrity when those I interact with can easily identify my values. Time to start again. Only then can I ask my own kids to live with integrity.

Step Three: Fostering Independence

Have you been supporting his independence in this area?

I haven't been supporting his independence. I do a lot of lecturing about his lack of responsibility and work ethic, but haven't provided him with opportunities or tools to foster those skills. Gosh, I still pack his lunch, wash all his sports gear, and clear his plates. I'm in charge of everything and I do everything because I think it will be easier and faster and I will get things done my way. I see the pattern here.

How will you foster your child's independence in a way that will influence this situation and ensure he is independent and self-sufficient when he is an adult?

- Stop talking down to him, lecturing, shaking my head in disappointment, muttering under my breath, or threatening.
- Become more encouraging, supportive, and accepting.

- Show him how to do all the things I have been doing for him and then let him practice without jumping on him for doing it wrong or not doing it perfectly.
- Set up privileges and responsibilities, so that I can be held accountable and not be allowed to change my mind if I am mad at him about something entirely unrelated.
- Follow through with agreements that we make and allow him to experience the natural consequences of his choices. This will be difficult, as I don't want him to fail and attend summer school, but if this is the course that must run, it won't be the end of the world.

Step Four: Living with a Teen

What can you do in the moment that will move the action forward without making things worse?

- Choose a more reasonable time to have a conversation with him—not at six in the morning when we're all getting ready to start our day.
- Use a more respectful tone, "firm and kind," as Vicki says, to let him know that I refuse to engage in power struggles with him.
- If I feel myself getting worked up, let him know that I need to have some time to calm myself down, so that I don't end up being disrespectful.
- Remember that I have done what I can to provide adequate study time and space. His choice to not do his homework is his choice. This is not my responsibility to make sure his homework is completed and he does not fail a class.

Step Five: Raising an Adult

What character traits or life lessons can you teach in this situation that will benefit your child from age eighteen to eighty?

Security: Instead of creating a safe place for Quinn to come with a failure or mistake, I became a very critical and demanding person in his life. I want to be a person he can trust with his challenges, concerns, mistakes, failures, and successes. This will only happen if I prove my faith in him with my actions and the way I speak to him. If I want him to have a sense of security in his life, it comes from him knowing he has what it takes to manage life and all its moving parts. That can't happen if I keep taking control away from him, so that I can have it.

Organization/time management: (Aha moment here.) Quinn has so many interests and things he is really passionate about. He is a natural athlete who enjoys playing one sport a season. He loves the team atmosphere and the hard work it takes to improve, and he looks up to the majority of his coaches. I would say his academic life is the least important to him, and I have been trying to force it to the top of his priority list. Instead of trying to rearrange what he cares most about, I could teach him time management and organizational skills so that he can balance all the areas of his life. These are certainly attributes that will assist him in his adult life, especially if he is going to continue to make the most out of every hour.

Responsibility: It's important for Quinn to learn responsibility, and I have been in his way without even knowing it. My getting angry and threatening to keep him home from his soccer game was not teaching him this lesson. It was teaching him that:

- I am unreliable, make empty threats, say one thing and do another, and do not follow through, so my words mean nothing.
- He can do whatever he wants and I'll bail him out, save him, or excuse his late homework so his coach doesn't bench him, all the while feeling bitter, resentful, and disappointed in him. I'm learning to take responsibility for myself in this relationship, and now I am clear on how to foster it in my child.

Step Six: Creating an Intentional Plan

Describe the routine, structure, or plan you want to implement.

Privileges and responsibilities: After learning about this concept from Vicki, a whole new world opened up for us. Instead of trying to force Quinn to do something or threatening him with punishments, this new connection leaves the control in his hands. We worked collaboratively to determine what responsibilities he must fulfill in order to enjoy the privileges that mean so much to him. Not only is this teaching Quinn more about accountability and time management, but it also freed up time for me to focus on more positive things with Quinn without overly involving myself in his business. It is allowing us to connect around other things, and that is making a change in our relationship already.

Homework (responsibility): Homework is done and passed in to teachers on time. If Quinn chooses to do his homework in the morning, it is up to him to set his alarm and give himself adequate time.

After-school activity or sport (privilege): If an assignment is missed or turned in incomplete, Quinn misses the sport/activity for that day until he completes the assignment.

Step Seven: Trusting Your Intuition

What do you know about your child that will ensure you have set up a structure that will work for him?

This kid wants to gobble life up. He has been like this since he could walk. He knows what he likes, what inspires and energizes him—and the list is long. He is also clear about what he doesn't like to do and the things that exhaust him. He tries to avoid these as much as possible. The kid works his fanny off for the things he loves but struggles to put that energy into the areas that have less meaning for him. If I remember that and stop thinking of him as lazy it will help me keep things in perspective. My guess is that he will do well in college because he will be able to pursue what he loves, and the same goes for his work life. Knowing this is going to make it much easier for me to accept the Cs on his report card.

CHAPTER THIRTEEN

Trials and Tribulations of Technology

The digital age is here, and like it or not, as parents we are required to help guide our children as they learn how to manage the technology in their lives in safe, thoughtful, and balanced ways. The method can provide guidelines for managing technology, while supporting independence in our kids and deepening the relationship we have with them.

School-Aged

Brittany and Robert are parents to nine-year-old Alice. When I asked them to share their thoughts on technology they said:

Screens are everywhere these days and it's hard to avoid them. We try not to overdo it with our daughter, but the truth is she has some screen time every day. And now that the kids are encouraged to use technology for school, it's hard to find a healthy balance. Technology slowly crept into our lives and we didn't take the time to set up any guidelines. We have resorted to making "on the fly" rules that we don't really enforce. As a result, Alice is starting to demand more and more screen time and getting fairly nasty if she doesn't get it.

As her parents, we try to explain the dangers of too much tech time, but we are met with resistance and nasty behavior, and just recently we found out that she has been using our devices without asking. It didn't occur to us that we were creating bad habits when Alice was three years old and we let her use our iPad at a restaurant to keep her amused so that we could talk. We can both see now that we created her idea that she could have access whenever and wherever she wanted. We are backtracking now and that's tough on everyone. We resorted to putting her on restriction recently and told her no more technology until...that's the problem, we have no idea how long to take it away from her. It's a mess.

Step One: Describing the Situation (in as few words as possible)

This is the result of the four questions you ask yourself to determine the mistaken goal of behavior.

Our nine-year-old wants access to more and more technology and is nasty and disrespectful when we say no. As a result, she has started sneaking our devices and we are fighting on a more regular basis. Frankly, I'm **angry** that she won't listen to us and abide by the rules we set in place. This tells me the mistaken goal of her behavior is **power.**

Step Two: Developing a Relationship Blueprint

Identify any negative labels you use with your children that influence their self-ideal.

I can get so angry with my daughter and use words like disrespectful, demanding and sneaky to describe her.

Replace the negative labels with positive attributes/qualities you want to use so your children develop a healthy self-ideal.

Thoughtful, responsible, honest, and accepting. Our relationship is pretty good, by and large. We enjoy each other's company as a family. Alice is close to her siblings. She is cooperative by nature, but ever since we introduced technology into the family, she has become more difficult to deal with. We'd like to reestablish a healthy and more respectful relationship so that we can enjoy the teen years, which are right around the corner. If we want Alice to develop a healthy self-ideal we are going to have to create a working list of attributes and qualities we know are crucial in healthy relationships. I think both my wife and I agree that this sounds so much more rewarding then spending our time fighting with our daughter.

What parenting strategies do you use to manipulate your children into changing their behavior and what will you replace them with?

We haven't created any guidelines for Alice, so we try controlling her access, threatening her with the loss of privileges if she keeps badgering us or we catch her sneaking our devices, and lecturing her about the dangers of too much technology time. When we consider that the strategies we use with her to deal with differences are the same strategies she will use in her adult relationships, it becomes easier to take this slow and put more thought into it. The first thing we are going to do is sit down and begin negotiating our positions and showing Alice about persuasive arguing, so she can make a case for herself. It means, of course, that we as her parents will have to keep an open mind and may even have to concede a few points if we want her to learn the power of the strategy.

What qualities of a healthy relationship do you want to focus on that, over time, will influence or change this scenario in a positive way and support qualities found in a healthy relationship?

Trust: We accuse Alice of being untrustworthy but when my wife and I talked, we realized that Alice couldn't really trust us.

- We don't follow through with what we say.
- We don't give our decisions much thought.
- We don't take her perspective into considerations when we make our parenting decisions.

We want to be able to trust her with technology and trust that she will tell us the truth, no matter how difficult it is. We want to trust that she can tell us anything and we will be on her side, but we haven't demonstrated that around technology—or anything else, for that matter. We can see that we have handled many other situations, like bedtime and sleepovers, in the same way. Our first priority is to start earning Alice's trust by demonstrating this value. This starts with following through on what we say, giving ourselves time to make thoughtful parenting decisions, and asking her questions and taking into consideration her perspective. Simultaneously, we will let her know we trust her more. Again, it is essential that our actions support our words. It will be difficult, but we will have to give her the benefit of the doubt and offer her space to make decisions and choices and wait and see what happens. Just talking this through makes it so obvious how this will improve every aspect of our lives.

Step Three: Fostering Independence

Have you been supporting her independence in this area?

We haven't been supporting her independence. We make decisions for her that we think are good for her. She is the youngest, so we tend to baby her and, as a result, she still shows a lot of juvenile behavior.

How will you foster your child's independence in a way that will influence this situation and ensure she is independent and self-sufficient when she is an adult?

- Use the Timeline for Training exercise to identify what self and home skills she can do on her own and then give her the space to master those skills.
- Identify the skill sets that require some training. We will offer her training and support and let her practice until she has mastered those skills.
- Talk with her about how much tech time seems reasonable to her and then come up with agreements that work for all of us.
- Give her a voice in the daily decision making and include her whenever it's reasonable.

Step Four: Living with a School-Aged Child

What can you do in the moment that will move the action forward without making things worse?

- Answer Alice's request for screen time clearly and confidently and not waver. If the answer is no, that is that.
- Revisit the agreement we have and let the agreement do the talking.
- When Alice starts to beg, plea, cry, or tantrum, our job is to stay calm and focused on our goal: to be consistent and committed and not feed the negative behavior.

Step Five: Raising an Adult

What character traits or life lessons can you teach in this situation that will benefit your child from age eighteen to eighty?

Resilience: We are clear now that we need to provide Alice with opportunities to bounce back when she doesn't get what she wants. We can't give in or give up on her or our agreements. We have to stay the course and trust that, over time, she will be able to bounce back quickly. We will offer her more responsibility so she can continue to struggle and overcome those struggles.

Confidence: We really thought we could boost our kids' confidence by telling them we think they are terrific. We both know that confidence is something that comes from the inside, not from the outside, but we did not know how to create that. If we want Alice to feel confident in her abilities then we are going to have to ensure she has lots of opportunities to try new things, participate in family policy, make her own decisions, and experience both the successes and the failures of really participating in life.

Step Six: Creating an Intentional Plan

Describe the routine, structure, or plan you want to implement.

Together the three of us created a schedule for Alice's technology time and we talked about how she would monitor her time and what would happen if she abused this new privilege. Now it's up to her to follow through with her end of the agreement and it's up to us to follow through with the consequences if she breaks it. As a result of this exercise, and recognizing that Alice was keen on the idea of boundaries that didn't change with our mood, we made more agreements in other areas of life that were beginning to cause a bit of stress for all of us.

Step Seven: Trusting Your Intuition

What do you know about your child that will ensure you have set up a structure that will work for her?

We know that clear boundaries and consistency from us support Alice's temperament. We thought that she enjoyed all the flexibility and spontaneity we provided her siblings, but nothing could be further from the truth. She is a much more settled child now that she knows the expectations. She knows we will follow through on what we say, so she is much more active in helping us create routines, structures, boundaries, and limits that support her growth.

Teens

Carrie says:

I feel like I haven't had a decent conversation with my son, Max, in a year. We gave him a phone last year for his fourteenth birthday and it's been downhill ever since. We tried to set rules around the phone, but they didn't really stick. Now he walks around the house looking down at his screen and he seems to have a chip on his shoulder. When I question him about the phone, he gets very defensive and nasty. I received the phone bill last week and became very upset. I was telling him how disappointed I was that he was being so irresponsible with his texting plan. Out of the blue, he called me a witch with a "b" and said he wished I wasn't his mother. I was crushed.

When I tell Max how hurtful he can be with his comments and his refusal to make eye contact with us when we speak to him, he just rolls his eyes, mumbles under his breath "whatever," and walks away. A few times I've taken the phone away because of his rudeness and disrespect. It's unacceptable and he needs to know that he can't go around talking to us that way. Last night I threatened to take his phone and he threw it against his bedroom wall. I've never seen him so angry. But what choice do I have? All kids have phones these days and I want him to have it so I can reach him but I'm tired of looking at the top of his head, paying his bills for him, and getting no appreciation or respect in return. I know he's smarter than this. I'm at my wits' end with this hurtful behavior and I don't deserve to be treated this way."

Step One: Describing the Situation (in as few words as possible)

This is the result of the four questions you ask yourself to determine the mistaken goal of behavior.

We recently gave my son a phone and he is abusing this privilege. He is not mindful of his texting plan and is not willing to pay for the extra charges. He is rude and distant from his family. I am **disappointed and hurt** by his behavior. I'm at a loss as to how to handle it, and as a result I've become equally rude and disrespectful in my reactions. Max is angry at the world and I'm concerned about the aggression that he has been showing lately. This tells me that his mistaken goal of behavior is **revenge**.

Step Two: Developing a Relationship Blueprint

Identify any negative labels you use with your children that influence their self-ideal.

The truth is I am very concerned about my son. I would describe him as distant, defensive, evasive, moody, ungrateful, rude, disrespectful, and indulged. I feel awful about seeing this list on paper.

Replace the negative labels with positive attributes/qualities you want to use so your children develop a healthy self-ideal.

Kind, flexible, caring, and courageous. Our relationship is shot, and if I want to repair it I know we have a long road ahead of us. There are some disconnects that I didn't even know were there. Honestly, I was shocked when I did this exercise and learned that Max's behavior was stemming from his belief that he "doesn't belong" or "isn't like/loved." I wanted to trace this back so I could figure out where I went wrong, and it didn't take long. I am going to start by reframing my ideas about my son. I am going to focus on his strengths and replace any negative thoughts with positive images.

What parenting strategies do you use to manipulate your children into changing their behavior and what will you replace them with?

I have been criticizing Max, either subtly or overtly, conveying that I didn't like the way he wore his hair, the clothes he likes, the shows he watches, or the way he played a certain game. I feel free to comment on the music he listens to and the friends he has and the way he handles situations. I am sure he feels like a complete disappointment to us. It makes sense that Max has shut down and is trying to avoid being hurt any further by pushing us away. I can imagine that Max might believe that I am trying to change him into the son I wanted instead of accepting the son I have. If I am honest, each time Max makes a decision contrary to the one I want him to make, I take it personally and use that as an excuse to lash out further at him. I didn't understand that was happening. I really believed I was supposed to influence him by commenting, editorializing, and critiquing every area of his life. Poor kid. I am going to begin by quietly observing. No more commentary from me. When I can be quiet and create some trust, then I will revisit the strategies that Vicki presented. I am not sure if I can be trusted to be quiet, and if I don't get this under control first, I will mess up everything else.

What qualities of a healthy relationship do you want to focus on that, over time, will influence or change this scenario in a positive way and support qualities found in a healthy relationship?

Acceptance: To think that Max felt like he didn't matter to our family is heartbreaking and completely understandable. When you have parents who comment on every aspect of your life, giving you feedback and sharing their opinions, how could you possible feel accepted? I know that I am a good mom and we have a solid family, but I can see now that I have sent the message to this child that I do not accept him for who he is. And I have to wonder, do I show acceptance in any areas of my life? I think I accept only the things that are in line with my beliefs and preference. If that is true, then I have a lot of work to do in clearing up what the true meaning of the word acceptance is.

In the short term, I can see that if Max believed that we accepted him for who he is and if he felt a strong sense of belonging in our family, we could avoid many of the unhealthy dynamics we are currently experiencing. I also know that as an adult, this is essential in any relationship. I don't want Max trying to prove his worth to anyone or putting up with anyone's constant criticism of him. I want Max to be in relationships with people who relish his company, who acknowledge his strengths and perspectives, and who support him as a person. And I want him to do the same for them.

Step Three: Fostering Independence

Have you been supporting his independence in this area?

It embarrasses me to admit that I have not been supporting Max's independence. I've been micromanaging him and expressing my disappointment and disgust in his attitude and behavior, and never stopped to try to figure out why he was acting that way. I have resorted to yelling, lecturing, shaming, and punishing—and that has only made the whole situation worse.

How will you foster your child's independence in a way that will influence this situation and ensure he is independent and self-sufficient when he is an adult?

- I will never say, "I'm disappointed in you" to my child again, no matter what.
- I will invite him into the decision-making process and implement his ideas so he knows he is being heard.
- I will focus more on Max's strengths and offer appreciations and encouragement. Our family is now holding weekly family meetings, and while at first Max seemed very apprehensive about giving and receiving appreciations, he is now a lot more comfortable with it and seems to genuinely like family meetings. Just removing the confrontational and hurtful talk has made a difference in his attitude, confidence, and independence.

Step Four: Living with a Teen

What can you do in the moment that will move the action forward without making things worse?

- Discovering the cost of the phone bill was the trigger in this particular case. I could have waited to talk to Max until I was calm, had my thoughts in order, and had some idea of a plan. Going at him in an overly emotional and worked-up state just made everything that much worse.

- It's true that it pushes my buttons when Max completely ignores me or seems evasive, so I could make an attempt to approach him in a less confrontational way: just a hug or pat on the shoulder, or a "Hey, buddy, I missed you today," an invitation to join in a game or activity, or an acknowledgment of a recent achievement. Even if Max doesn't make eye contact or respond, he will hear the respect in my voice and that is what matters in that moment. It's up to me to let go of my thinking, "Why is he treating *me* like this?" I understand now that the behaviors of being rude and not answering, not making eye contact, and mumbling can all be addressed later just by rebuilding trust in this relationship.

Step Five: Raising an Adult

What character traits or life lessons can you teach in this situation that would benefit your child from age eighteen to eighty?

Accountability: I want my son to learn how to operate in a world filled with technology in a respectful manner. I see adults all over the place and their faces are glued to their phones or iPads and they are not having actual conversations with the people standing next to them. Part of the privilege of having a phone at this age, for Max, is his accepting that we will hold him accountable for his actions and for him to balance his desire to be texting and his need to make eye contact and interact with the people around him. Accountability is a trait that will benefit him now and as an adult, as he will have the ability to take responsibility for his choices and actions and the positive or negative consequences those may bring.

Growth mind-set: I know this is a new concept everyone is talking about, but as I learn more about it and apply it to my own life, I can see that anyone who develops a growth mind-set is going to have a much better chance at creating and sustaining a life of meaning and deep satisfaction. The growth mind-set supports taking healthy risks, reaching out, working hard, and being open minded and flexible, which are all attributes I hope Max embodies as an adult. And I want my son to become a man who appreciates progress and improvement and never worries about perfection or pleasing others. We are, after all, dynamic individuals in a constant state of change, trying and failing, bettering ourselves, picking up the pieces, and starting that process over again.

Step Six: Creating an Intentional Plan

Describe the routine, structure, or plan you want to implement.

Before we even talked about the phone bill or phone in general, I apologized and let my son know that I am on his side. I told him that I've been going about showing him that in the wrong way. I thought he needed discipline and tough love in order to learn tough lessons. Now I know this is not what he needs. He needs to know that we're a team and that there is nothing he could do that would cause me to stop loving or believing in him. I find that he is more receptive now because he doesn't feel attacked.

Phone agreement: Max earns a bit of money mowing lawns and doing odd jobs in the neighborhood and will contribute 50 percent of his income to his phone bill each month. He is 100 percent responsible for paying any overage charges accrued from too much texting. If he is unable to pay it, the phone is shut off until his debt is paid back.

Max has agreed to have a few blocks of time during the day (in the morning before school and the hour leading up to dinnertime) when his phone is out of sight and he "disconnects." This has allowed us to "connect" and to increase the quality of our interactions.

Step Seven: Trusting Your Intuition

What do you know about your child that will ensure you have set up a structure that will work for him?

He is a thoughtful kid who now has his eye on fairness as a result of our treating him in hurtful ways, albeit unintentionally. He thrives when we encourage him and show appreciation for his contributions to the family. Without it he questions his abilities and his standing in the family. Talking with him on a regular basis in a calm and loving manner helps Max feel safe opening up to us and sharing his perspective. The more he shares and feels listened to, the more confidence he exhibits.

> **Note from Dad:** I know that Max was hurting and that through the rebuilding of our relationship, I am noticing a change in him. He seems more willing and able to have a conversation with me, share details about his day, and the other day he even came to me with a problem. That hasn't happened in a few years, and I was so thankful that he felt comfortable enough to share it with me. He is starting to trust that his mistakes or failures do not define him in my eyes. I am striving to view successes and failures in the same way and let him know that as long as he puts forth an effort that's all that matters. I love him no matter what.

Afterword

I believe, with all my heart, that the method I have been using for the past twenty-five years with my own children and with the tens of thousands of parents I have worked with can be used by anyone who is willing to go through the sometimes messy moments that come with trying something new. Although the method is made up of only four elements with specific questions designed to help parents flush out the critical clues , it will take practice and patience on your part to get the most out of it. With practice comes familiarity, and with familiarity comes confidence.

The Straight Talk on Parenting is a labor of love. For twenty-five years I have been steadfast in my belief that parents and their children are the true experts in their lives and that they have what it takes to experience the same results that they would if they hired an expert. If parents are given the same tools and resources to use that we in the field of parent education have at our disposal, there is no reason they won't facilitate change. I also believe that it is my responsibility as an educator to instill in parents a sense of confidence in their ability to do what I do, as well as to teach them the same method I use for making positive changes in families. My hope is that one day parents will look in the mirror before they look to an outside source for the answer, and ask, "What's really going on here?" When this happens, I believe there will be shift in the way we parent. Confidence facilitates change.

Index

About the Author

Vicki Hoefle is a professional parent educator, author, parent coach, and national speaker with over twenty years of experience teaching parents, educators, and caregivers how to raise respectful, responsible, and resilient children. Hoefle combines her expertise in Adlerian psychology and as an International Coaching Federation certified coach to bring parents sustainable and proactive parenting strategies that provide time-tested tools for harvesting a happy and peaceful family life. *Straight Talk on Parenting; A No Nonsense Approach on How to Grow a Grownup* is Hoefle's second book; she is also the author of *Duct Tape Parenting: A Less is More Approach to Raising Respectful, Responsible and Resilient Children* (August 2012.) Her informative and highly engaging presentation style keeps her in demand as a speaker, facilitator and educator. Hoefle is a mother of six and lives in Middlebury, Vermont. For more information, visit www.vickihoefle.com.